**Speaker's Corner Books**

is a provocative new series designed to stimulate,
educate, and foster discussion on significant public
policy topics. Written by experts in a variety of
fields, these brief and engaging books should be
read by anyone interested in the trends and issues
that shape our society.

More thought-provoking titles
in the Speaker's Corner series

Think for Yourself!
An Essay on Cutting through the Babble, the Bias, and the Hype
Steve Hindes

The Enduring Wilderness:
Protecting Our Natural Heritage through the Wilderness Act
Doug Scott

Parting Shots from My Brittle Bow:
Reflections on American Politics and Life
Eugene J. McCarthy

The Brave New World of Health Care
Richard D. Lamm

God and Caesar in America:
An Essay on Politics and Religion
Gary Hart

For more information visit our Web site
www.fulcrum-books.com

Ethics for a Finite World

an Essay Concerning a Sustainable Future

Herschel Elliott

Fulcrum Publishing

Golden, Colorado

Library of Congress Cataloging-in-Publication Data
Elliott, Herschel.
    Ethics for a finite world / Herschel Elliott.
        p. cm.
    Includes bibliographical references.
    ISBN 1-55591-545-0 (pbk.)
    1. Ethics, Evolutionary. 2. Environmental ethics.   I. Title.
BJ1311.E45 2005
171'.7--dc22

                                                                2005015984

ISBN 1-55591-545-0

Printed in the United States of America
0 9 8 7 6 5 4 3 2 1

Editorial: Sam Scinta, Katie Raymond
Cover and interior design: Jack Lenzo

Fulcrum Publishing
16100 Table Mountain Parkway, Suite 300
Golden, Colorado 80403
(800) 992-2908 • (303) 277-1623
www.fulcrum-books.com

Contents

Foreword .... *ix*
Preface .... *xxv*
Acknowledgments .... *xxix*
Introduction *1*
A Commentary on Important Terms *9*

Chapter One:
The Factual Refutation of Moral Theories **13**
    Moral Beliefs as Theories about How Human Beings
        Can Live on Earth 14
    A Darwinian Assessment of Ethics 15
    The Environmental Principle 18
    Factual Limits on Moral Behavior 19
    The Moral Obligation to Prevent Immoral Acts 20
    The Evolving Nature of Ethics 22

Chapter Two:
A Critique of Western Ethics **24**
Characteristics of Western Ethics 25
    A Survey of the Assumptions of Western Ethics 26
        The Intrinsic Worth of Every Human Being 26
        Value as Cumulative 26
        The Moral Goal of Maximizing Value 27
        Human Beings and Their Moral Standing 27
        The Purely Instrumental Value of Everything Else
            on Earth 27
        Equal Justice and Human Equality 28
        The Moral Irrelevance of Individual Differences 28
    Human Rights in Western Ethics 29
        The Right to the Necessities of Life 29
        The Right of Religious Freedom 29
        The Right to Employment 29
        The Right to Found a Family 30
        The Right of Asylum 30

Moral Duties in Western Ethics 30
    The Duty to Prevent Human Suffering and to
        Save Human Lives 30
    The Duty to Prohibit All Discrimination
        and Favoritism 30
The Categorical Nature of Western Ethics 31
Ethics for a World of Unlimited Resources 32
Ethics for a World of Limited Resources 33
The Factually Necessary Condition for Western Ethics 34
The Failure to Recognize the Contingent Nature of
    Moral Knowledge 35
Summary 37

Rationalism in Ethics 38
What Is Rationalism in Ethics? 38
The Logical Form of the Refutation of Rationalism
    in Ethics 40
The Contingent Consequences Caused by Enforcing
    the Principles of Western Ethics 41
The Logical Origin of Rationalism in Ethics 44
A Summary of the Errors of Rationalism in Ethics 51
Reason and the Rule of Law 52
Interpretation as Confirmation 59
Summary 60

The Fallacy of the Naturalistic Fallacy 61
The Circularity of the Assumption That a Gulf
    Separates Values from Facts 63
Dual Domains of Value and Fact 64
Ethical Theories as Speculation 66
The Distinction between Types of Empirical Knowledge ...69
The Method of Conjecture and Refutation 72
Seeing-As and Seeing-Truly 73
A Thought Experiment about Moral Theories 76
The Empirical Basis of the Knowledge of Ethics 77
Environmental Ethics and the Naturalistic Fallacy 79
Summary 80

The Failings of Personal Ethics 81
    Personal Ethics and Moral Law 83
    The Error of the Belief That Moral Laws and Principles
        Are Universal and Certain 83
    The Error of Disregarding the Nonpersonal Human Agencies
        That Determine Human Behavior 85
    The Inability of Personal Ethics to Address the Physical
        Causes of Human Ills 89
    Summary 91

Chapter Three:
The Fundamental Principles of an Ethics for a Finite World 93
    Two Kinds of Value 95
    Trade-Offs and Materially Dependent Values 97
    Points of Moral Reversal 98
    Nature's Veto of Moral Theories 102
    Ethics as Biocentric 103
    Equal Membership in the Moral Community but
        Not Equal Status for All Members 104
    Moral Constraint as an Essential Condition for
        Moral Life 106
    Human Actions, Not Human Genes, as the Warrant
        for Human Rights, Duties, and Opportunities 108
    Contingent Rules for Moral Behavior 109

Chapter Four:
Proposals to Further the Goals of Ethics 110
  1. The Global Village Is a Self-Negating Ideal 112
  2. Nations and Peoples Make Their Own Moral-
      Cultural Experiments........................... 115
  3. Immigration Is Strictly Limited................... 117
  4. The Importation of Fuels, Timber, and Minerals
      from Other Nations Is Restricted................. 119
  5. To Reduce an Excessive Population Is Morally More
      Difficult than to Reduce Excessive Consumption 122
  6. All Citizens Get Coupons for a Year's Ration of
      Petroleum Fuels 124

7. Taxation Is a Tool for Attaining Environmental
    and Societal Goals 125
8. Government Loans to Students Pay for Public
    Education; Students Repay Them when They Join
    the Labor Force 128
9. Vegetarianism Repairs Environmental Damage and
    Improves Human Health 131
10. A Significant Causal Link Is Established between
    Those Who Receive Health Care and Those Who
    Pay for It. 133
11. Governmental Offices Sell Basic Foods at World
    Wholesale Prices. 134
12. Advertising Is Curtailed to Reduce Consumption and
    to Secure a Durable and Resilient Environment 135
13. A Nation's Climate and Environment Are
    Recognized as Affecting Citizens' Behavior 136
14. A Low Population Density Allows a Maximum
    Quality of Life 138
15. There Is No Optimal Population and No Correct
    Way for People to Live in a Finite World 141
16. The Average Workweek Is Reduced 143
17. Unearned Capital Gains Do Not Belong to
    Individuals; Rightfully, They Belong to Society 144
18. Invested Money Earns No Interest 146
19. The Environmental Principle Suggests a
    Nonegalitarian Conception of Justice 147
20. Different Nations and Societies Use Different
    Methods for Reducing and Controlling
    Their Populations. 148

Endnotes 152

Foreword

This is a revolutionary book. Revolutions come in various forms, some more affirmed and sustained by history than others. George Washington was a revolutionary, as was Karl Marx, and while Washington's ideas survived the judgment of time, Marx's ideas couldn't be sustained and were found fatally flawed. So might the ideas of Herschel Elliott. But I believe his thinking is of immense importance and needs to be debated widely. I believe he is the first scholar who deeply and thoughtfully looks at the implications to ethics of the new world humankind is increasingly being confronted with.

I.

"In every age," writes Jacob Bronowski in *The Ascent of Man*, "there is a turning point, a new way of seeing and asserting the coherence of the world." Similarly, in 1862, Abraham Lincoln said, "As our case is new, we must think and act anew. We must disenthrall ourselves, … "

It seems clear that the great forward leaps of human progress have been made by people who "disenthrall" themselves and develop "a new way of seeing and asserting the coherence of the world." We see this in Galileo and Copernicus, who had the audacity to claim the Earth was not the center of the universe. We see this in Charles

Darwin, who took on the religious establishment with the heretical idea that man was a product of evolution. We see it in political systems, where John Locke and Thomas Jefferson had the revolutionary ideas that people could govern themselves. We see it in Freud, with his upsetting idea that man was not always a rational animal. All of these people challenged the current ordained wisdom of the time and all of them proved correct.

These people were labeled heretics. Their ideas were aired amidst great controversy. Aldous Huxley once observed, "All great truths begin as heresy." Humankind falls into a routine way of viewing the world and then, breaking the continuity, someone observes that the current orthodoxy is at variance with reality. A great debate ensues. New ideas are upsetting. Attempts are often made to shout down new opinions. If the idea is grounded in reality, the heretical idea eventually prevails and becomes accepted wisdom. One generation's heresy is frequently the next generation's orthodoxy, which thus sets the stage for the next new heresy. New ideas replace old ideas, but often only after a struggle. This is as it should be. The poet Robert Lowell observed, "New occasions teach new duties. Time makes ancient good uncouth."

The great earthshaking controversies of our history—between science and religion, between church and state, between Freud and traditional thinking—have all been initiated by people who were characterized as heretics for challenging the straightjacket of orthodoxy. New ideas come particularly hard in public policy. Public policy is reactive and new problems are addressed as long as possible with old solutions. It has a hard time adjusting itself to new ideas. As Barbara Tuchman observed:

Policy is formed by preconceptions and by long implanted biases. When information is relayed to policy makers, they respond in terms of what is already inside their heads and consequently make policy less to fit the facts than to fit the baggage that has accumulated since childhood.

In the same spirit, John Stuart Mill wrote:

When society requires to be rebuilt, there is no use in attempting to rebuild on the old plan ... no great improvements in the lot of mankind are possible, until a great change takes place in the fundamental constitution of their modes of thought.

II.

Who are the modern prophets whose heresies will turn into tomorrow's truths? We know they are there, but we differ strenuously on who they are. Some would say Julian Simon and others Paul Ehrlich. Every person would have his or her own list. "We see the world not as it is, but as we are," goes an old aphorism. We choose our prophets because they lead where we already think we are going. Like beauty, contemporary prophets are mainly in the eye of the beholder. It is only the future that vindicates our choices. Contemporary assessment of new ideas is so notoriously flawed that tradition teaches us that "prophets are without honor in their own country."

Elliott may be one of those prophets. He has had the courage, intellect, and audacity to take on many of the orthodox assumptions of our age. We will look back from the future and recognize the growing importance of his message.

III.

I may be wrong, but I believe that time and logic are on Elliott's side. I suggest there is massive and mounting evidence that we live on the upper slopes of some awesome logarithmic curves. The "new way of seeing and asserting the coherence of the world" in our time is to show that infinite growth cannot take place in a finite world. I choose not to repeat all the depressing statistics.

I believe that when the history of these times is written, it will show our prophets were those recognizing and confronting the finiteness of our world. Each year our population grows, the deserts creep, pollution seeps, and forests shrink, the globe warms, our topsoil erodes. Habitats degrade and more and more species disappear. We are in the hinge of history, where ethnocentrically we thought the Earth belonged to us, but ecologically we are finding out, to our great astonishment, that we belong to the Earth. We are finding that human genius can push the limits of nature but that, ultimately, man cannot conquer nature but is subject to its timeless, inexorable laws.

Recently, no less an authority than the Pentagon issued a report, "An Abrupt Climate Change Scenario and its Implications for U.S. National Security," that stated chillingly:

> Abrupt climate change is likely to stretch [the Earth's] carrying capacity well beyond its already precarious limits. Disruption and conflict may well be endemic features of life. ... Every time there is a choice between starving and raiding, humans raid.

Despite the massive and growing evidence that we are causing unprecedented harm to our ecosystem, a vast number of people choose to ignore it. No one today can "prove" global warming will inevitably act in a harmful way, and there will always be an optimist somewhere who will relate that increased temperatures will ultimately be good for humankind. There are always congenital optimists telling us against all evidence that a negative is actually a positive. It is this type of conflict that too often paralyzes public policy. We cannot know with absolute certainty, so we do nothing. Ken Boulding observed that the essential human dilemma is that all our experience is in the past and yet all our decisions relate to the future. That makes dramatic change hard to accomplish. In absence of proof of the negative, we are forever hopeful:

> Our images of the future themselves are affected by our evaluations of them. We tend to put too high a probability on futures that we like and too low a probability on those that we dislike.

Elliott believes that Garrett Hardin's "The Tragedy of the Commons" is one of the most important essays ever written. James Gleick, in his book *Chaos*, states, "The world awaits the right metaphor." He points out that, no matter how smart we are, we often cannot see something without the correct metaphor.

IV.

"Some people believe that there cannot be progress in Ethics, since everything has already been said. ... I believe the opposite. ... Compared with the other sciences, nonreligious ethics is the youngest and least advanced," stated Derek

Porfit in *Reasons and Persons.*

Elliott challenges us with what some will consider the ultimate heresy: that ethics are relative, relative in the sense that while ethical claims have an objective, factual status, those ethical statements differ according to the circumstances in which they are made. The ultimate judge of our ethical codes must be Mother Nature. This will likely disrupt your standard way of thinking, but ask yourself, what if, just what if, global warming is a reality and expanding human activity is causing irreparable harm to our ecosystem? What if a growing economy and growing human numbers require us to confront limits? What if it was hubris, not reality, to think that we are the only species that can grow without limits? Would not this require us to rethink the very basis of much of our ethics? What would this mean to our cherished concepts of individual and human rights? How would the emergence of ecological limits alter our long-held ethical beliefs?

One of *Science* magazine's most cited articles give us one alternative. Hardin's "The Tragedy of the Commons" postulated that when natural resources are held in common, free and available to all for the taking, the incentives that normally and naturally direct human activity lead people to steadily increase their exploitation of common resources until they are exhausted. Each person, group, or nation keeps all the benefits and immediate advantages resulting from its exploitation, while everyone in the world shares almost equally in the harm that exploitation causes. Every participant in the tragedy pleads "not guilty," but the entire system moves inextricably to disaster. The incentives all push us toward destruction. Perhaps with our oceans warming, our ice caps melting, our fisheries depleting, our rainforests disappearing, our coral degrading, it is time to debate the ethics of the commons.

Our standard of living, our economic system, our political stability require expanding use of energy and resources; and much of our political, economic, and social thinking assumes infinite expansion of economic activity with little or no restraint on resource use. We all feel entitled to grow richer every year. Social justice requires an expanded pie to share with the less fortunate. Progress is growth, and the economy of all developed nations requires steady increases in consumption. What if such a scenario was unsustainable? How does the world live with finitude?

I suggest this would be a Copernican world where much of our economy and our social systems would have to be rethought. Would it not also cause us to rethink and reconceptualize much of our ethical obligations? Our ethics and concepts of human rights have been formulated in a thought-world, the world of Kant and a priori reasoning. Reason alone dictates our ethics and they discard all physical constraints and assume an infinite world.

But what if our thought-world ethics started running into the world of limits. What if there was a tragedy in the commons where double-entry bookkeeping applied and one person's or one country's gain was someone else's loss? Ecological limits would make much of our moral thinking obsolete. We would actually be required to repudiate some of our historic ethical beliefs and to alter many of our basic political and economic institutions.

Historically, our moral thinking has been set in the domain of abstract thought and reasoned judgment. Traditional ethics assume an infinite world. But in a world of finitude, ethical behavior must not only make moral sense but ecological sense. No ethics can demand what the ecosystem cannot support. We cannot ignore the real world consequences of our abstract beliefs.

Take, for example, Elliott's criticism of human rights. Human rights are often claimed to include positive rights, which generally require the expenditure of resources. Negative rights restrain government and don't require resources. The government can't abridge our speech or tell us how to pray. Positive rights suggest that we collectively have a duty to provide more food, more housing, more medical care, and more social services to a growing number of people worldwide. Wherever in the world a child is born, that child has some inherent human rights, which others must provide. In a finite world, such demands eventually lead to the asymptote of the collapse of the ecosystem.

Elliott logically claims that we cannot have a moral duty to supply something when the act of supplying it further harms the ecosystem and makes life on this Earth unsustainable. We cannot disregard the factual consequences of moral behavior. If acting "moral" causes further compromise to the ecosystem, that "moral" behavior must be rethought. Ethics cannot demand resource use that the ecosystem cannot tolerate.

You may passionately believe that there are no limits and that population growth and economic growth can go on forever, but you must also consider whether you are wrong. Elliott asks, "What if ethical behavior had to be not only rational but also ecological?" No ethical code can demand of human's duties and behaviors that which nature cannot support. Moral codes, no mater how logical or well reasoned, and human rights, no matter how compassionate, must be capable of being practiced within the limitations of a finite ecosystem. Moral life cannot be constructed solely in a thought-world: it has to also make ecological sense.

For most types of moral behavior that occur in a finite commons, there are points of moral reversal where well-meaning actions cause further destruction of the ecosystem. Every new fishing boat in an overfished commons adds to the destruction. What creates wealth at the beginning (additional food from the ocean) at some imperceptible point in time turns destructive (overfishing a limited commons). In Elliott's world, assets turn into liabilities and virtues become harmful. Elliott agrees with Oxford philosopher Derek Parfit that moral philosophy will continue to evolve, and suggests that some of today's "virtues" may not survive the ultimate challenge of making ecological sense.

V.

I know and am sobered by the fact that there has been a myriad of Cassandras predicting doom that has not taken place. We know from thoughtful study of history that most doomsayers (and most utopians) have been wrong. Will and Ariel Durant, after a lifetime of studying history, observed that ninety-nine out of every one hundred new ideas that come at a society are bad ideas. It has been very stabilizing to societies and nations to give heavy burden of proof to those arguing for dramatic change. History shows, as a group, they are usually wrong. Most prophets, alas, have been false prophets.

VI.

That said, I suggest that the next major revolution in human thought will be where humankind confronts the finite. It will be the revolution in science, public policy, and human consciousness. It will assert that infinite growth cannot take place in a finite world and that our atavistic thoughts, our large and growing population, and the way our economy is currently structured will be found obsolete and dangerous to the survival of humans on Earth. It will bring about a new wave of seeing and of asserting the coherence of the world.

Commenting on the worldwide crisis that humanity confronts, anthropologist Van R. Potter said:

> The extreme novelty of humans as the dominant force on this planet is as surprising as is our current rate of destruction of our own habitat and that of the earth's other life forms. This disregard is all the more striking since, in geological terms, our species has only recently departed from its 'place in nature.' The full implications of our derivation by the random processes of biological evolution in a mere 5 million to 7 million years from an animal much like a chimpanzee have yet to be incorporated in any manner into the fundamental beliefs or institutions of our own, or in fact, any society. In its very success, our species has raised grave problems that demand new kinds of solutions. Will we, by better understanding the processes that made us what we are, grow in capacity to solve the frightening problems of the future arising from our very selves?

Note some of Elliott's iconoclastic conclusions:
1. Because they are misconceived, some theories give rise to problems that are insoluble. Western egalitarian ethics is one such theory. It both encourages and supports an ever-

increasing population and an ever-growing world economy. In a finite world, such growth is logically impossible. Hence, any ethics that allows or even tolerates continual growth is doomed to fail.

2. The flaw of Western ethics is its assumption that moral laws and principles are justified by transcendental means—either by appeal to the infallible word of God and/or by appeal to reason. Such nonfactual, a priori, criteria justify moral laws and principles that are universal and infallible. So conceived, they cannot be limited or refuted by the factual consequences that they cause when they guide human affairs in a finite world. In effect, they make moral life irrelevant to life on Earth.

3. The fatal flaw of this ethics is that it is impossible in principle to limit or to sacrifice any human interests in order to maintain the Earth's biosystem—a system that living things have created and sustain.

4. Fundamental to an ethics for a finite world is the environmental principle: to preserve the endurance and the resilience of the Earth's system of living things. This principle cannot be justified by appeals to reason or to the infallible revelations of God. It also cannot be justified by valid inferences from a human-centered definition of value or from human-centered moral principles that are merely postulated. Furthermore, it cannot be refuted by the fact that it conflicts with public opinion or the world's great moral traditions. Finally, it is not subject to scholarly rebuttal by professionals in moral philosophy. In contrast, the environmental principle has a biological necessity. Any ethics that

denies it allows people to destroy their environment's ability to support them. Such an ethics contradicts itself in the sense that to obey its commands causes an environmental breakdown and thereby makes it impossible to obey its commands. Thus, the environmental principle has an intercultural objectivity. It is proved by the absurdity of its denial.

5. The environmental principle uses the indirect and empirical method for justifying moral behavior. It discards what does not work and retains what does. Hence, there are no final moral answers. Nature never tells people what they ought to do, but it does alert people to what they cannot do. Nature has the final veto over the moral laws and principles that people propose to live by. The fact that factual evidence can refute moral theories makes the knowledge of ethics fallible but amendable, open-ended, and cumulative.

6. Because factual evidence can nullify value judgments and moral theories, facts and values fall in the same domain. No gulf separates them; no conceptual gulf makes moral judgments distinct from factual judgments. The so-called naturalistic fallacy is itself a fallacy.

7. An ethics for a finite world has a factual foundation. Human beings can only propose the moral laws and principles they will try to live by. Nature either tolerates these human proposals or it denies them. Nature is the final determinant of the ethics that is capable of directing human affairs in a finite world.

8. Western ethics typically discriminates against all who break moral law; it discriminates against thieves, murderers,

and all who commit immoral acts. It restrains them by force, if necessary. It certainly does not give them equal rights, freedoms, and opportunities. Just as Western ethics does not subsidize or reward people for theft, murder, greed, and sin, so an ethics founded on the environmental principle cannot subsidize or reward people for their reproductive or their environmental transgressions. It must discriminate against those who deny it—those who destroy their environments, those who fail to curb their reproductive behavior. Human activities—not human genes—determine the rights, freedoms, and opportunities that are morally possible. Inevitably, people who either ignore or defy the environmental principle will cause their rights, freedoms, and opportunities to be restricted or curtailed.

9. In the physical sciences, there is no algorithm by which factual data can be turned into scientific or theoretical knowledge. The data that contradict the consequences entailed by a scientific theory render that theory false. Supporting data can only tentatively confirm a theory; they cannot establish its certainty or universal truth. The situation is similar for ethics. There is no algorithm by which factual data about human behavior can generate knowledge about the correct ethical theory. Supporting data only show that nature tentatively allows an ethical theory. Contrary data, however, prove what people cannot do; they can demonstrate that a moral theory is counterproductive, that it is absurd, that it is false.

10. Ethics builds on the principle of moral reversal. Behavior can produce great benefit for mankind when human populations are small and environmental resources plentiful. But

the same behavior can cause moral tragedy or disaster when populations are excessive or when environmental destruction has made vital resources insufficient to satisfy vital human needs. As Hardin noted, in ethics, quantities matter; numbers are morally significant.

That, dear reader, is a very new and different way of looking at the world.

VII.

This revolution in thought will be more contentious than any that has gone before. There is in the Western world a deep-seated cultural belief in abundance, and that a world of plenty is the natural state of affairs. Shortages are seen to be caused only by a lack of imagination and appropriate technology. The developed world enjoys its lifestyles and the underdeveloped world seeks to emulate these lifestyles. But increasingly, we are finding a new upsetting reality that is at variance with our cultural assumptions.

We are increasingly finding that the oceans cannot endlessly absorb pollution nor the atmosphere the gases of our industries. We are finding that resources are not unlimited; topsoil is too often ephemeral. We are schizophrenic about our technologies—we marvel at them but we realize that they are not always benign and often come close to being a Faustian bargain. We are finding that economic growth increasingly has by-products that may cause more harm than the good incorporated by the product.

VIII.

These concerns will be a new chapter in "seeing and asserting the coherence of the world." Where past genius was recognized for pushing back these limits, future genius will be recognized on how to adapt to the very rapidly approaching limits inherent in living in a limited ecosphere. More accurately, we must both push back these limits and learn to live within the clear overall limits.

When I was nineteen, a wise person told me "maturity is a recognition of one's limitations." It was hard for me to accept—I had a typical nineteen-year-old's desire to read every book, travel to every country, hold every job, live every experience. But truth won out and maturity was a recognition of my limitations.

So also, I suggest, with the world. We know that no trees grow to the sky, that no species of animal can grow without restraint, and that the harbingers of ecological destruction warn daily of a new set of limits.

IX.

According to the studies of Professor Al Bartlett from the University of Colorado, the current rate of population growth would suggest that in 300 years, human activities would put about as much thermal power into the Earth's atmosphere as the sun puts in! The absurdity of this situation is obvious. Independent of the greenhouse effect, global warming from this direct heating would likely render the Earth uninhabitable long before the passage of fourteen doubling times.

—Richard D. Lamm

Preface

Some problems are difficult to resolve because their complex causal chains are interwoven and tangled. Other problems are difficult to resolve because they are mistakenly conceived. Indeed, their misconception makes them insoluble. The moral problems of the modern world are, I believe, of the second type. They cannot be resolved as long as moral knowledge is held to be justified by nonempirical and transcendental criteria. That is, they are insoluble if the infallible word of God is taken to state the authoritative laws and principles for moral behavior. They are also insoluble if valid inferences from a human-centered definition of value and from moral principles that are merely hypotheses are used to justify an ethics of universal human rights and the equal treatment of all members of the human race.

When egalitarian moral principles are conceived to be a human birthright, every individual has the same right to food and vital necessities, to the same freedoms, and to the same prospects for a healthy and satisfying life. In effect, these moral ideals apply to all people regardless of the number of children they have, regardless of whether parents can provide for their children, and regardless of how severely people have damaged the environment that supports them. When such moral convictions direct human affairs, they subsidize the status quo of exponential growth both in the human population and in the human exploitation of natural resources.

Exponential growth logically entails a doubling time for any quantity. A few doublings produce enormous numbers. William B. Dickinson notes typical examples: in 550 years, a growth rate of 1.9 percent per year will produce a population of one human being per square meter of the dry land on Earth, excluding Antarctica; in 1,620 years, it will produce a human population whose mass equals that of the Earth.[1] Obviously, the human population will stabilize at much lower numbers. If not, it will deplete environmental resources and cause its own collapse.

Inevitably, an ethics for a finite world must be a steady state ethics. It must build on the moral obligation to assure that the human population does not grow and that the human exploitation of the world's lands and physical resources is maintained at sustainable levels. If an ethics of equal justice and universal human rights does not add principles that control both the human population and human resource use, it will cause the environment to break down and end all prospects for moral life.

In the early 1970s, when I first read Garrett Hardin's essay on the tragedy of the commons, I was struck by the startling cogency of its simple-seeming argument. I recognized at the time that it was iconoclastic—that somehow it nullified both the Christian and the rationalist traditions of Western ethics. The major thrust of his argument is inescapable: behavior that is selfish and self-centered, as well as behavior that is altruistic and self-sacrificing, produces the same tragic result. Human beings, whether they are directed by selfish or by altruistic ideals, follow the disposition— built into the genes of all living things and reinforced by the moral codes of present human societies—to increase both the human population as well as its exploitation of available resources. Unless societies can impose and enforce deliberate constraints on human behavior, they will cause a destructive exploitation of the environmental commons that supports moral life. In effect, a factual state of affairs can nullify any system of ethical beliefs that people propose to live by.

Hardin's argument demonstrates the biological basis of ethics. Because moral theories change the course of events in nature, they must pass empirical tests. Nature can allow an ethics to be practiced under some circumstances, but it can cause its practice to die out under others. Indeed, no moral theory is viable if its practice causes its extinction. It simply is not suited to direct human behavior in a finite world. The fact that empirical evidence can refute moral beliefs proves the methodological assumption to be false that moral knowledge can be justified nonempirically by an appeal to divine revelation or to human reason. Inevitably, moral knowledge is a type of empirical knowledge. It is open-ended and cumulative. Its goals are twofold. The first is to maintain an enduring and resilient world ecosystem. Then, after the environment is secure, its secondary goal is to devise human societies that will make human life ever more worth living.

It has taken me, Lo!, these many years to construct a theory of ethics grounded in Hardin's insights. This book is my attempt to construct a coherent theory of ethics that builds on the fact that moral beliefs are merely hypotheses. All ethical theories are subject to nature's veto.

xxix

Acknowledgments

Although they may disagree with some of my assumptions and conclusions, I would especially like to acknowledge my debt to Virginia Abernethy, John Tanton, The Federation for American Immigration Reform (FAIR), and Richard D. Lamm. Their encouragement has enabled me to keep working on the method and principles of an ethics that can control the human population and its destructive exploitation of the Earth's natural resources.

I have found support for my moral concerns in the articles and books by Virginia Abernethy, especially *Population Pressure and Cultural Adjustment* and *Population Politics: The Choices That Shape Our Future.* While she was editor of *Population and Environment,* she encouraged me to keep writing by publishing a number of my essays. Her excellent editorial judgment removed inconsistencies and unnecessary diversions.

I want to thank John Tanton. His invitations to the writers' workshops every October have provided valuable contact with many people, both liberal and conservative, who are troubled by the problems caused by a runaway human population and by the destructive exploitation of the Earth's resources.

I also appreciate the yearly meetings of FAIR, which provide factual information about the measures that now prevent a resolution of the population and environmental problems of the modern world. FAIR also gives details of the steps that many are taking to resolve them.

Richard D. Lamm has been a constant source of encouragement. He champions many of my ideas. He worked with me to write a joint article, "A Moral Code for a Finite World."[1] His encouragement has kept me writing about an ethics that is appropriate for an overpopulated world with a damaged and deteriorating environment.

Finally, I would like to thank Giovanna Holbrook, for giving me the opportunity to stay at Selva Verde Lodge in Costa Rica to work full-time on organizing various essays into this book.

Introduction

I consider Garrett Hardin's "The Tragedy of the Commons" to be one of the great essays of the twentieth century. [1] It demonstrates that any ethics is absurd if it either allows or requires moral behavior that produces tragic consequences. The purpose of this book is to unfold the implications of the undeniable and iconoclastic principle that factual evidence can refute any ethical theory that proposes to direct human affairs in a finite world.

Hardin's seminal essay demonstrates that incentives for growth are built into all normal human activities. When people act in their own self-interest, or even when they act in the unselfish and philanthropic interest of all mankind, their actions almost invariably increase the exploitation of the land and resources that are held in common, free to everyone for the taking. Typically, the benefits of the exploitation accrue to specific individuals or groups, while the damage caused by that exploitation is shared almost equally by everyone and everything within the commons. The lack of causal connection between those who benefit from exploiting the commons and those who pay the costs of its exploitation gives rise to an increasingly destructive abuse of common resources.

Furthermore, Western ethics builds on the principles that human rights are universal and that the humanitarian duty to aid all in need is unconditional. It assumes that modern technology will find the resources necessary to sustain growth, both in population and in the production of material goods and services. As a world-dominating species, human beings continually diminish the competition from all other living things. Few natural constraints remain to keep them from exploiting all common resources until they are depleted. Now, only human-imposed constraints can prevent mankind from increasing its use of land and natural resources until their scarcity causes the environmental commons to collapse to a simpler, pioneer state incapable of supporting the civilization that caused the collapse.

Although Hardin's is one of the most frequently cited essays in the journal *Science*, a central thesis of his essay is continually overlooked and ignored. The fact that a tragedy of the commons is possible proves that empirical evidence— a factual state of affairs—can refute an ethical theory. Thus, the error of Western ethics is to be found in the belief that a priori, transcendental, or at least nonempirical criteria can justify its human-centered, egalitarian, and supposedly universal moral principles. By contrast, an ethics suited to a finite domain must recognize that there is a physically necessary condition for its practice: namely, that land and natural resources be available to support it. Whenever the excessive human exploitation of the Earth's resources begins to cause the environment to deteriorate, from that time on, all ethical theories must build on the factual necessity to limit the human population and to reduce the human use of material resources to quantities that an enduring and resilient ecosystem can sustain. Any ethics that fails to do so drastically diminishes the support capacity of the environment and threatens to cause it to break down to a pioneer state incapable of supporting the ethics that brought about the moral tragedy. Such an ethics is self-eliminating. It must be corrected or discarded.

At present, the factual evidence of rapid environmental decline is there for all to see, unless they are not prevented from doing so by custom or moral conviction. It includes global warming and climate change; the melting of glaciers and the polar ice caps; the destruction of the prairie ecosystem of central North America; the ongoing decimation of the tropical forests of the Amazon, West Africa, and Southeast Asia; the sullied water of almost all lakes and rivers; the near collapse of ocean fisheries; and the smog that envelops the world's large cities. These phenomena bear witness to the destructive effects of modern human activity. They can be seen as the consequences of a growing population and a runaway economic system maintained by the destructive exploitation of the world's natural resources. Without a rapidly imposed and drastic limit on the human use of the world's land and natural resources, present human activity can only lead to a tragedy of the commons.

It took hundreds of millions of years for nature to create the stock of petroleum, mineral wealth, and biological diversity that mankind recently has learned to exploit. Only for a limited time can modern civilization continue to squander nature's finite capital. Long before all of this capital is gone, two defining aspects of the modern way of life will prove to be unsustainable. First, the multinational version of corporate capitalism that is dedicated to the perpetual growth of the production of material goods and services will falter. Second, the human-centered ethics, which is dedicated to the universal rights and moral obligations of everyone in a steadily growing human population, will prove to be self-refuting.

To elaborate the first point: as the Earth's natural capital is spent down, the profits from economic production can no longer be invested to finance the exploitation of more land and natural resources. Profits can no longer be used to build the manufacturing facilities needed to create more jobs, expand infrastructure, and produce more consumer goods and services. When nature can no longer tolerate the further human exploitation of the Earth's lands and capital resources, the people of the rich industrial nations will have to revise—downsize—their way of life. A steady increase in economic production will no longer be available to pull the increasing billions of the world's poor into the state of security and prosperity enjoyed in the modern industrialized and urban societies. Capitalist economics will become a steady state system, or it will falter and become extinct.

To elaborate the second point: as the Earth's stock of natural resources is depleted, the focus of moral life can no longer be human centered. That is, the moral goal cannot be to meet all human needs, to relieve the suffering of billions of the world's poor, and to assure equal justice and equal opportunities for all members of an expanding human population. To be specific, moral behavior can no longer be directed toward growing more food; creating more jobs; building more low-cost housing; expanding municipal water and sewage-treatment plants; constructing a greater infrastructure of highways and parking lots; making medical care available universally; finding cures for AIDS, malaria, and other devastating diseases; building and staffing more schools, libraries, and research facilities; or setting aside more parks and nature preserves where city residents can find relief from the hubbub of urban life. The Earth no longer has the land and material resources necessary to satisfy the physical demands of the steady growth in population and in economic production—which the principles of Western ethics validly entail.

When faced with a scarcity of land, water, fuel, and natural resources, more compassion, greater moral effort, more sacrifices, and an equal sharing can do nothing to create more of these vital necessities. They can do nothing to alleviate the poverty and inequities caused by overpopulation and environmental degradation. The Earth no longer has the resources that allow an expanding human population to satisfy, with equality and justice for all, its expanding material needs. Unfortunately, this will be true especially for the hundreds of millions of the most needy who live in the shantytowns surrounding many of the world's megacities.

In short, the error of Western ethics is to attribute persistent human need and suffering to the moral failure of the citizens of the wealthy nations to make the sacrifices necessary to lift the world's poor out of poverty. As long as an egalitarian ethics entails the moral obligation to give philanthropic aid without conditions, it will subsidize the status quo—a steady increase in the population and a steady increase in the exploitation of the Earth's limited lands and natural resources. Eventually, continual growth will so degrade the world environment that it will be physically impossible to support the practice of this ethics.

The argument in support of an ethics for a finite world has four parts. In chapter one, the task is to establish the environmental principle and the empirical nature of ethics. The Darwinian explanation for the evolution of species suggests a similar explanation for the evolution of social behavior. Human moral conduct is only a special case of the conventions that direct the behavior of all social animals. Human societies can only propose the conventions that they will try to live by; nature either tolerates their proposals or it denies them. The physical necessity to maintain the durability and resilience of an evolving ecosystem makes the knowledge of ethics incomplete and conditional. Inevitably, nature—not a rational argument from the human-centered definition of value and from moral principles that are merely assumed— is the final determinant of the ethical theories that can guide human behavior on this finite Earth.

In chapter two, the task is a critical one: to point out the conceptual and methodological errors at the foundation of Western ethics. The first section lists moral principles and human rights that are not subject to empirical refutation. The second section shows the inadequacy of rationalist methods for justifying moral theory. The third section demonstrates that to maintain the naturalistic fallacy is to make it impossible for empirical evidence to refute a moral theory. And the fourth section details the deficiencies of an ethics conceived as moral rules for personal behavior.

As long as moral theory uses nonempirical and ratio-nalist methods to justify universal human rights and moral principles, it cannot resolve—indeed, it is likely only to exacerbate—the present destructive exploitation of the Earth's finite resources.

Chapter three has a constructive task: to state the prin-ciples that are suited to direct moral behavior in a finite world. It builds on the environmental principle—the factual necessity of assuring the endurance and resilience of the Earth's system of living things. It requires both physical and biological constraints on moral behavior. There are eight corollary principles that help maintain a durable and resilient environment. The goal of these principles is to reduce the human population as rapidly as possible and to stop the destructive exploitation of the Earth's natural and biological resources.

Chapter four has a practical task: it lists many of the proposals that environmentalists commonly advocate. It also suggests new ones, and it calls for thinking up an indefinite number of others. However, all proposals require empirical evidence to test whether they further or thwart the goals of moral behavior in a finite world.

The fact that a proposal wins the approval of the majority of voters is not an appropriate test because voters often disregard long-term societal and environmental needs. Similarly, proposals that support a larger human population or an increase in the production of consumer goods and services may win majority approval but fail objective environmental tests; they may destabilize society or put the environment in jeopardy.

There are no final moral answers. Nature never tells people what they ought to do; but it does alert people to what they cannot do. Nature always has a veto over the moral laws and principles that people use to guide their lives. The indirect empirical method of sloughing off what does not work and retaining what does makes the knowledge of ethics cumulative and open-ended.

No ethical theory can tolerate moral behavior that allows a scarcity of resources to force people to abandon their moral ideals. It is a moral duty for people to live within the support capacity of their national boundaries and for them to maintain an ample margin of safety. Clearly, both the size of the human population and the quantity of material resources that human beings utilize work together to alter the rules for moral behavior. Human rights and moral obligations are a function both of population density and of the support capacity of environments.

An ethics for a finite world has three basic tasks: (1) It must enforce the environmental principle and secure the endurance and resilience of the world's biosystem, which sustains moral life. (2) It must discover how to simplify human material needs and lessen the human demands on the environment. (3) Then, after the environment is secure, it must structure society so that citizens can expand the social, aesthetic, cultural, and intellectual values that make human life ever more worth living.

A Commentary on Important Terms

Empirical Truth

Scientific theories and empirical generalizations are said to be true when all known empirical data support them. They are false and must be revised or discarded when factual data are found to refute them. Theories are only confirmed indirectly by means of their deductive consequences. In effect, the factual data that confirm the predictions of one theory confirm all theories that entail the same predictions. Inevitably, general and theoretical empirical knowledge is tentative and conditional. It cannot be final.

Valid Claims and Self-Evident Truth

Claims are valid if they correctly unpack information already contained in the grammar, definitions, and premises assumed. Because it is a contradiction to assert the premises of an argument and deny a conclusion that it validly entails, valid claims have a necessity that no empirical data can refute. They cannot be partly valid and partly invalid. They cannot flip-flop from valid to invalid according to the shifting consensus of peer opinion. Valid claims are logically necessary; they are analytically or self-evidently true.

The statement that all squares have equal sides is an example of a statement that is analytically or self-evidently true. It would be bootless to spend time and effort searching to find a square with unequal sides, for, by definition, there are none. This case illustrates the fact that empirical data cannot limit or refute a self-evident truth.

The Two Kinds of Knowledge

The two different criteria of truth noted above yield two different types of knowledge. Some knowledge falls in the nontemporal domain of valid claims and self-evident truths. Other knowledge is about physical objects, events in the physical world, and their properties. It falls in the conditional domain of empirical knowledge.

The Domain of Certain Knowledge

As long as statements simply unpack the information given by the definitions, postulates, and assumptions, they belong in the domain of certain knowledge. In this domain, the validity of conclusions guarantees that they are universally, timelessly, and necessarily true. The validity of statements, however, cannot guarantee that they have an empirical referent or a practical application. For instance, a valid Euclidean theorem may attribute properties to lines and figures that are factually false for straight lines that are defined as lying on the surface of the Earth. Whenever the theorems of plane geometry refer to actual objects and figures on Earth, they make contingent factual claims; they no longer belong in the domain of certain knowledge.

The Domain of Empirical Knowledge

It is essential to understand the indirect method by which empirical knowledge is gained. General and theoretical statements about physical objects, events, and their properties begin as hypotheses. Valid inferences are essential to their confirmation. Empirical theories are verified tentatively when empirical data confirm the claims that they validly entail. If, however, factual evidence proves that an inference—validly inferred from the definitions and assumptions of a theory—is false, then it is logically necessary that the theory that entails that inference is itself false. Empirical knowledge is the residue of generalizations and theories for which no factual data, as yet, have been found to refute any claims that they validly entail. The indirect method of confirmation makes empirical knowledge subject to correction but cumulative.

The Rigorous Distinction between Validity and Truth
Arguments about important economic, political, and ethical claims are often vitiated by the false assumption that their validity establishes their truth—their appropriateness for directing the course of events in the physical world. As noted above, a theory or a set of assumed premises may entail valid conclusions that are, in fact, false. It is a serious logical error to confuse a proof of validity with empirical confirmation. Clear and careful thinking must never allow the term "valid" to mean "correct," "confirmed by observed data," or "true."

An Infinite Class
An infinite class is defined as one in which there is a one-to-one correspondence between its members and the members of a subset of itself. For example, a given line contains as many points as a segment of itself that is half as long. Similarly, an infinite universe contains an infinite amount of every resource even though that resource makes up only a fraction of the matter of the universe. An infinite material universe can no more run out of mineral or energy

resources than the number series can run out of numbers.

The hypothesis that the solar system has an infinite quantity of material and energy resources available for human use promotes the hubris of unlimited human control over events in nature. Because an infinite domain makes all shortages of energy or minerals logically impossible, apparent shortages can only be temporary or local. Thus, if the resources available for human use are infinite, material scarcity cannot prevent the capitalist economy from steadily increasing the production of material goods and services. Indeed, when the natural capital of an infinite world is used to pay annual interest, people can have the value of their investments increase exponentially. In a world with unlimited land and resources, even a Ponzi scheme[1] can work. There can be no overpopulation and no limit to economic growth in an infinite world.

Chapter One

The Factual Refutation of Moral Theories

All moral beliefs are theories about how human beings affect the course of events in the physical world. In effect, they make an implicit prediction. They predict that moral behavior will produce benefit rather than harm or disaster. No one can know in advance what the future factual data will be. People can only observe and record. Factual data may support or confirm their predictions. But factual data can also deny or refute them. Human beings must be humble before the fact of what happens in the physical world.

Western ethics has not yet recognized or accepted the moral consequences of the Darwinian revolution. Human beings cannot know the final truth about how human behavior, even moral behavior, will change the course of events in nature. Behavior that accords with moral theory may produce much benefit under some factual conditions. But under other factual conditions, that same type of behavior can cause an ecosystem to break down and societies to die out. The contingency of the consequences caused by moral beliefs refutes the established opinion that moral knowledge has a unique, nonempirical status that gives its laws and principles a universal authority that is categorical and final.

Two facts about human moral behavior are morally significant. One is the fact that human societies only propose the moral rules that its members live by. The other is that nature decides whether to tolerate human ethical proposals or to deny them. Together these facts entail the environmental principle: the obligation of an ethics for a finite world to maintain the durability and resilience of the ecosystem that makes moral life possible.[1] The certainty of this principle is not justified by reason and valid arguments. Rather, its proof is given by the moral absurdity of its denial. This principle establishes the empirical foundation of ethics for a finite world.

Moral Beliefs as Theories about How Human Beings Can Live on Earth

When people act as their moral theories direct, they change the course of events in nature. Inevitably, moral theories make factual claims. Thus, they have to be tested—confirmed or refuted—by what they cause to happen in the world when they direct human affairs. Clearly, they are useful when they produce much benefit and little harm. Just as clearly, they are absurd and counterproductive when they produce little benefit or cause much harm, or even disaster. Indeed, moral beliefs and ethical theories are refuted when they subvert the purpose of moral life: when they cause an environment's breakdown and thereby render moral life impossible, or when they destabilize society and thereby diminish the quality of human life. Knowledge of ethics does not belong in the domain of a priori certainty and self-evident truth. Clearly, it falls in the domain of empirical knowledge.

A Darwinian Assessment of Ethics

All social animals live by conventions that regulate the behavior of the members of the group. Most species of animals that nature has devised over the past billion years have failed and have become extinct. Similarly, it is likely that most of the behavior patterns animals have used to regulate their social life have also failed; they have been replaced by others that better promote the group's welfare and survival. This Darwinian assessment applies equally to human behavior. Moral theories and beliefs are only proposals about how people can live in society and in finite and evolving environments. By allowing the deficient and defective practices to die out, nature selects those that survive.

In "The Last Americans," Jared Diamond states, "Because peak population, wealth, resource consumption, and waste production are accompanied by peak environmental impact—approaching the limit at which impact outstrips resources—we can now understand why declines of societies tend to follow swiftly on their peaks."[2] His assessment of the environmental cause of the decline of civilizations clearly supports the Darwinian thesis that all human moral theories are subject to empirical refutation. Accordingly, we, in the modern world, live by moral conventions that nature still tolerates. But it cannot be expected that moral evolution has stopped. It cannot be the case that present moral conventions describe correct moral behavior for all times and all circumstances. Moral principles and theories have to be tested continually. Nature either permits them for a while or it repudiates them. Nature—not valid reasoning from human-centered moral assumptions—is the final judge of the moral conventions and the ethical theories that are able to direct human behavior in a finite world.[3]

Some human societies have practiced cannibalism. It doubtlessly seemed as natural and necessary to cannibals to kill and eat people who were not members of their tribal society as it presently seems to be natural and necessary for people to kill and eat animals that are not members of human society. In the 1960s, the English comedians Donald Swan and Michael Sanders had a very popular record, "At the Drop of a Hat." It included the following parody of a moral argument: the son of a cannibal chief returns from study abroad. The chief takes affront at his son's outrageous proposal to outlaw cannibalism; he argues that if the Great Juju had meant for us not to eat people, he would not have made them of meat. The outraged chief goes on to add that to give up eating people would upset the whole internal economy. How can we plan our meals if we don't eat meat? What else but meat is there to eat?

The chief's outrageous moral argument in support of cannibalism is relevant here because it parodies the equally arbitrary argument in support of the modern meat-based diet. The claim that only human beings have moral status allows people in the modern world to say that cows, sheep, goats, pigs, and chickens are made of meat, whereas human beings and their pet dogs, cats, and horses are not. Indeed, vegetarianism would upset the global economy and change the nature of modern life.

The fact remains, however, that the essential difference between the ethics of modern meat eaters and the ethics of cannibals is in the arbitrary definition of what living things have moral status and what do not. What is *not* arbitrary is the kind of diet that an enduring and resilient environment can sustain for different populations. The Earth does not have the resources to support a meat-eating diet for the present 6 billion people, nor for the projected 9 to 12 billion people that will need to be fed by the end of this century. The finitude of the Earth makes it inevitable that the greater the number of people in the world, the more vegetarian the human diet must become.[4]

Many other examples illustrate the different moral conventions that human societies have tried to live by. For centuries, slavery supported a ruling elite, and kings claimed a divine right to rule. By means of sacred rituals and texts, a priestly class long maintained dominance over the lives of the masses. Today, professionals, entertainers, and the chief executive officers of large corporations either already possess unearned fortunes or receive wages that are many hundred times greater than those of the typical worker. Their vast wealth allows them to have lives of luxury supported by workers whose minimal wages keep them in virtual slavery. Indeed, present political and economic conventions give to the superwealthy great power, privilege, and leisure. It is highly likely that such modern conventions cannot stand the test of time.

In the modern world, multinational corporations determine how most of the world's people live. The momentary ascendancy, however, of the conventions of global trade and corporate free-market capitalism is no proof that mankind now possesses the final knowledge of the principles that order human affairs. Rather, when considered from the evolutionary perspective, modern conventions are nothing other than the latest theory about how human beings can behave toward one another, how they can organize society, and how they can treat the plants and animals within the Earth's community of mutually dependent living things. The ethical theory of the modern world may well prove to be as faulty and ephemeral as the previous ethics of cannibalism, of the divine right of kings, of slavery, or of rule by a priestly caste.

The Environmental Principle

The definitions and assumptions of Western ethics evolved in a world of ample natural resources. In a world of virgin lands, untapped forests, fertile soils, and ample water, fuels, and mineral resources, there are few constraints on human ideals and aspirations. In such a world, the people of pronatalist religious and ethnic groups can move to new lands whose resources can support the growing population. In such a world, refugees and immigrants need not crowd into places that are already fully settled. In such a world, democratic governments; technological innovations in agriculture and medicine; the free-market, corporate, capitalist system; and global free trade allow continuous economic development to produce an ever-greater abundance of material goods and services. High-interest rates can reward invested capital, which, in turn, increases the efficiency of labor and expands production. Indeed, in a world of vast, open lands and undeveloped resources, a growing economy can lift the world's impoverished billions into the mainstream of industrial well-being.

However, now that the limited resources of the Earth are being exploited so rapidly as to threaten an environmental breakdown, the finiteness of the world imposes a necessary condition on moral life. It can be stated as the environmental principle. The first duty of moral behavior is to preserve the endurance and the resilience of the Earth's system of living things. This principle cannot be justified by appeals to reason or the infallible revelations of God. It cannot be justified by valid inferences from a human-centered definition of value or from moral principles that are merely assumed. Furthermore, it cannot be refuted by appeal to public opinion or to the great moral traditions of the Western world. It is not subject to scholarly rebuttal by professionals in moral philosophy. Rather, it has a physical and biological necessity. If an ethics denies the environmental principle, it directs all people who practice it to destroy their environment's ability to support them. Such an ethics is doomed to fail because those who live by it simply die out. It contradicts itself: to obey its moral commands creates a situation in which it is physically impossible to obey its moral commands. Thus, the environmental principle is proved by the absurdity of its denial. It is the fundamental principle of an ethics for a finite world.

Factual Limits on Moral Behavior

Conditions of an impending and intractable scarcity severely limit the types of moral behavior that are possible. They also change the kinds of moral behavior that are suited to the different environments in which they occur. For instance, if vital necessities are abundant, the rules of moral behavior can be right for everyone. But if these necessities are in short supply, everyone cannot follow those same rules. One cannot give food equally and fairly to all who are starving when there is not enough food to go around; the biscuit that one person eats is denied to all others. In effect, moral theories are unsustainable—even dangerous—if they require moral behavior that constantly increases the exploitation of the Earth's finite land and natural resources until the resources of the environmental commons are exhausted. It is nature—not a conclusion validly entailed by an anthropocentric definition of value or assumed moral principles—that determines whether a moral theory succeeds or fails. If human moral behavior should cause the environmental commons to break down, that breakdown is clear, factual evidence of moral failure. The natural resources of any environment limit the human rights, freedoms, and duties that are possible for people living in that environment.

It should be noted that a cosmic accident—such as the one that probably caused the extinction of the dinosaurs—does not refute the environmental principle. Such a collision merely demonstrates that life on Earth is fragile and ephemeral. An environmental disaster that is not caused by human activity is not evidence of moral failure. It does not affect the universality of the environmental principle.

The only questions that can arise about the need to enforce the environmental principle are ones of timing. When will human beings so exploit the Earth's finite resources that the environmental commons that sustain them will begin to break down? How long can human ingenuity and modern technology postpone the onset of intractable scarcity in a finite world? When will the human exploitation of land, water, energy, and biological resources begin to cause the rapid decline of the Earth's biosystem? Whenever a scarcity of land and resources becomes unavoidable, the environmental principle must be enforced. To enforce it is the only way to overcome human suffering and moral tragedy, the only way to fulfill the purpose of moral life.

The Moral Obligation to Prevent Immoral Acts
Western ethics discriminates against everyone who breaks moral law; it discriminates against thieves, murderers, and

all who commit immoral acts. It restrains them by force, if necessary. It certainly does not give them equal rights, freedoms, and opportunities. Similarly, an ethics founded on the environmental principle has to discriminate against those who trash their environments and those who fail to control their reproductive behavior. It does not give them equal rights, freedoms, and opportunities. The environmental principle prevents human rights from applying to all human beings universally and without discrimination. It also denies that the obligation is unconditional to render humanitarian aid to all in need—no matter what the causes of that need are and no matter what the consequences of the gift of aid may be. Inevitably, people who either ignore or defy the environmental principle must be restrained. Their rights, freedoms, and opportunities need to be curtailed. They may forfeit their right to philanthropic aid as well.

Just as Western ethics does not subsidize or reward people for theft, murder, greed, and sin, so an ethics founded on the environmental principle cannot subsidize or reward people for their reproductive or environmental transgressions.

Admittedly, it will be very difficult to decrease the human population and to require everyone to use only a limited ration of the natural resources of the Earth's commons. It will also be difficult to reign in the capitalist economy, dedicated as it is to the ever-expanding production of consumer goods and services and to the need to pay interest on invested capital. But either mankind will find the means to accomplish these monumentally difficult and environmentally necessary tasks, or it will fail. It fails if it allows the egalitarian principles of a human-centered ethics to subsidize a steady population growth. It fails if it allows the global capitalist system steadily to expand the production of material goods and services. Any such failures would be factual evidence of moral error—the denial of the environmental principle.

The Evolving Nature of Ethics

Human beings cannot create moral systems that are universally necessary or self-evidently true. Basically, they can only propose the moral laws and principles they will try to live by. Nature then either tolerates the human proposals or it refutes them. Inevitably, an ethics for a finite world has a factual foundation. Nature is the final determinant of the ethics that is capable of directing human affairs in a finite world.

Once it is understood that moral behavior changes the course of events in nature, it follows that the moral behavior that a moral theory makes morally obligatory can cause unknown and unexpected consequences. If that behavior should disrupt society or put the environment in jeopardy, the ethical theory that requires that behavior is counterproductive. It is futile; it is mistaken.

In the physical sciences, there is no algorithm by which factual data can be turned into scientific or theoretical knowledge. Supporting data can only tentatively confirm a theory: they cannot establish its certainty or final truth. Contradictory data, however, prove that a generalization or theory is false: they require that it be modified or rejected. Inevitably, scientific knowledge is both incomplete and evolving.

The situation is similar for knowledge of ethics. There is no algorithm by which factual data about human behavior can generate knowledge about the correct ethical theory. That is, factual data cannot establish the truth of any ethical theory. Supporting data only show that nature tentatively accepts it. Contrary data, however, prove what people cannot do; they show that a moral theory is counterproductive, that it is absurd, mistaken, false. The method of proposal and possible rejection makes the gaining of knowledge in ethics an open-ended and evolving process. It can never be certain; it can never be final.

Chapter Two
A Critique of Western Ethics

Chapter two has the critical task of assessing Western ethical principles and the a priori (or at least the nonempirical) method by which they are justified. The critique will be that Western ethics builds on two errors. One is a misconception of the nature of ethics; the other is the mistaken use of a priori reasoning—reasoning that factual evidence cannot refute—to justify moral laws and principles. Thereby, it falsely judges moral claims to be universal in scope—unaffected by population density or environmental collapse.

Western ethics appeals to reason, conscience, the coherence of unbiased and considered human moral judgments, man's spiritual nature, and/or the infallible word of God to yield knowledge of ethics. So conceived, however, ethics falls in the hypothetical domain of a priori knowledge. There it concerns only the ideal—not what actually happens in the physical world. When sequestered in the a priori domain of valid arguments and self-evident truth, moral knowledge becomes universal and certain. A case in point is the Declaration of Universal Human Rights of the United Nations of December 1948. It illustrates the universal and unquestioned authority of moral principles. These principles are commonly held to govern the behavior of individuals and to determine national and international policies as well.

As long as moral knowledge is sequestered in the hypothetical domain of nonempirical thought, it is impossible in principle for factual evidence ever to refute the valid conclusions from moral theory. Consequently, many people brought up in the Western ethical tradition are nonplussed by the assertion that ethical beliefs are subject to factual refutation. It seems inconceivable to them that nature can repudiate moral laws and principles. Yet this is exactly the case: human beings can only propose how they will behave in society and how they will use the resources of their finite environments. Nature either tolerates their proposals or it vetoes them. Faced with nature's veto, any societies that stubbornly cling to the a priori certainty of their moral principles simply die out and take their hallowed moral theories with them.

Characteristics of Western Ethics

Before we can assess Western ethics and its use of rationalist or a priori methods to justify moral claims, it is necessary to note the principles, rights, and duties of this ethics. No claim is intended that everyone in the Western world accepts them all. And no attempt is made to reconcile these principles with the claims and counterclaims of professionals in moral philosophy. The only claim is a factual one: the following principles underlie the moral decisions commonly made by most people in the Western nations, by democratic governments, and the United Nations.

It is evident that few of these principles are ever consistently enforced. Indeed, whenever they entail absurd consequences, they are conveniently overlooked or forgotten. Furthermore, failure is often thought to be built into their very nature because they are commonly held to be lofty ideals that no one can expect ever to be fully realized. In any case, the majority of the people in the Western nations never seriously question the moral authority of the following assumptions. Whether one is liberal or conservative, atheistic or devoutly religious, these principles commonly guide both personal behavior and public policy.

It is also evident that when they guide human behavior, these moral principles and duties cause factual consequences. They include the moral obligation to aid all children, refugees, and people in need, regardless of the human or personal causes of their plight. Thereby, they incorporate incentives that subsidize population growth and necessitate a steady increase in the exploitation of the world lands and natural resources. But they include no penalties or moral disincentives that limit such growth. Consequently and inevitably, on this finite Earth they lead to the breakdown of the Earth's biological commons and to the demise of the ethics that caused the tragedy.

A Survey of the Assumptions of Western Ethics

The Intrinsic Worth of Every Human Being

Every human life is precious. The assumption that every human being has intrinsic worth underlies all arguments for outlawing abortion, capital punishment, and euthanasia for the terminally ill. The loss of any human life is a loss of value in the world. Murder, genocide, and crimes against humanity are commonly considered to be the ultimate moral evil.

Value as Cumulative

Intrinsic values are not diminished by the existence of other values; hence, they are additive. More always has greater value than less.

The Moral Goal of Maximizing Value

Because every human being has intrinsic value, to increase the human population maximizes the amount of value in the world. Moral behavior should also maximize the instrumental values of goods and services that people want. Growth is always desirable. Growth is a moral ideal.

Human Beings and Their Moral Standing

Greek rationalism plus Jewish, Christian, and Muslim monotheism make human beings absolutely unique in the world. They differ from all other living things in that they have moral standing. In effect, moral rights, principles, and duties apply only to human beings, for they alone have moral significance.

The Purely Instrumental Value of Everything Else on Earth

Human beings are the locus of value. All other things on Earth—the land, natural resources, plants, animals, and even the environment—lack intrinsic worth. They have moral significance only as means to human ends. Thus, the activities of harvesting timber, draining wetlands, or killing other animals for food, convenience, medical experiment, or sport cannot be prevented or limited unless, directly or indirectly, they harm human beings or their interests.

Furthermore, for those ensconced in the human-centered assumptions of Western ethics, the environment has moral significance only if people can be educated to respect it and to value it. In effect, the environment has moral significance only if human beings can be motivated through free will to give it a human-dependent value.

Equal Justice and Human Equality

The fact that all human beings are members of the human race makes them share all the essential or defining human characteristics equally. When moral equality is taken to be a defining characteristic of all human beings, many moral claims follow by valid deduction. For example, the second paragraph of The Declaration of Independence declares, "We hold these truths to be self-evident, that all men are created equal, that they are endowed by their creator with certain inalienable rights, ... " The only way that such a moral claim can be self-evidently true is for moral equality to be one of the defining properties of the human species.

If, however, it is self-evident that all human beings are morally equal, then it is a contradiction to deny it. Indeed, to deny it would be like denying that all squares have equal sides. Hence, as long as human beings are defined as moral agents with equal moral status in the hypothetical domain of a priori thought, the principles of equal justice and equal human rights are self-evident, universal in scope, and true under all circumstances. Their certainty is a logical consequent of a moral definition.

The Moral Irrelevance of Individual Differences

Once the principles of moral equality and equal justice are assumed to be essential or defining characteristics of all human beings, all nonessential differences between individuals become morally irrelevant. For example, the diverse characteristics of human individuals—their health; intelligence; knowledge; discipline; individual effort; reproductive restraint; stage of life; the capacity of their environments to supply their needs; their culture and national origin; and their religion—cannot alter universal human rights or diminish the individual's prospects for a satisfying life. Furthermore, from the definition of moral equality it is easy to deduce that the fetus, the newborn, the child, the adult, the senior citizen, and the moribund all can expect equal justice to give them the same human rights. Indeed, as long as moral equality and equal justice are considered to be defining properties of all who are genetically human, the accidental or nonessential human characteristics cannot limit or deny moral laws and principles.

Human Rights in Western Ethics

The Right to the Necessities of Life
Equal justice gives human beings universally and without discrimination the right to adequate food, clean water, housing, education, sanitary facilities, and health care. These rights hold no matter what the personal or environmental causes of the human need may be; they also hold regardless of the societal or environmental tragedy that the fulfillment of these rights may cause. The mere fact of human need and suffering activates the universal human right to the necessities of life.

The Right of Religious Freedom
All people have the right to believe and to practice the religion of their choice.

The Right to Employment
All adults have the right to employment within the global economy; they have a right to wages that will allow them to buy the necessities of life.

The Right to Found a Family
As the United Nations Charter on Human Rights proclaims, all adults have an equal right to found a family and to choose the number of children they will have. Because it can validly be inferred from the principles of human equality and equal justice, the human right to reproduce is logically necessary and universal; it cannot be abridged by facts—by the inability of the parents, the society, or the local environment to support them.

The Right of Asylum
All true refugees who flee death and persecution in their native lands have the fundamental human right to find refuge in another country.

Moral Duties in Western Ethics

The Duty to Prevent Human Suffering and to Save Human Lives
The principles have been noted that all human beings have intrinsic value, that intrinsic values are cumulative, that the moral goal is to maximize the amount of value in the world, and that moral equality and equal justice require an equal sharing of the world's lands and natural wealth. Thus, the moral obligation stands to do everything possible to save human lives, to prevent poverty from degrading human life, and to render philanthropic aid to all in need.

The Duty to Prohibit All Discrimination and Favoritism
The principles of moral equality and equal justice require that all human beings be given equal consideration and equal opportunities. They entail the corollary duty to ban all discrimination, bias, and preferential treatment among human beings.

The Categorical Nature of Western Ethics

The universal principles, human rights, and moral duties of Western ethics are usually assumed to concern only the ideal; they describe only what ought to happen in the world, not what actually does happen. In any case, there is little doubt that in the Western world most people and most professionals in moral philosophy consider the knowledge of ethics to be a unique kind of knowledge. It is assumed to be unconditional and universal in its application to all mankind. To those ensconced in the ideal and nonempirical nature of ethics, it seems to be a categorical mistake to say that factual evidence can refute or limit a moral theory. As long as the laws and principles of ethics remain in the hypothetical domain of a priori knowledge, they have an authority and universality that cannot be limited by expediency or factual evidence. The fact is, however, that their truth in the domain of a priori thought gives them no empirical certainty; indeed, it gives them no necessary relevance to the course of events in nature.

As an example, it is common to criticize a person's questionable behavior as not just unwise or inexpedient but, decisively, as being immoral. A similar assumption presupposes that infallible moral principles can determine whether or not human cloning is immoral and, hence, whether or not it should be made illegal.

The belief in the uncompromising certainty of moral claims is nicely summarized in John Rawls's *The Theory of Justice*: "Each person has in inviolability founded on justice that even the welfare of society as a whole cannot override."[1] In a later summary he asserts, "Being first virtues of human activities, truth and justice are uncompromising."[2] A similar belief in the unconditional certainty of moral principles is to be found in the work of Peter Singer. In the chapter "One Community" of his recent book *One World* he writes, "America's failure to pull its weight in the fight against poverty is, therefore, due not only to the ignorance of the American public but also to the moral deficiencies of its political leaders."[3]

Ethics for a World of Unlimited Resources

The human-centered principles of Western ethics evolved when the human population was small and scattered, when vast areas of the world were open for human exploitation. In that world, scarcity could not constrain human ideals and aspirations. All shortages were local. If people lacked anything, either they had to learn better to exploit their resources, to trade their surpluses for what they needed, or to move to new lands.

In general, when land and resources are unlimited, there can be no physical causes for human need or poverty. Ignorance, laziness, and the neglect of humanitarian moral duties are the sources of human suffering. In an infinite world, human failure is the cause of human ills.

Undoubtedly, to live by the principles of Western ethics in a world of seemingly unlimited natural wealth has been conducive to human survival and human well-being. Furthermore, the belief in a universe of ever-ample resources allows people to continue to assert that a growing economy and a renewed dedication to the principles of universal human rights and equal justice for all mankind will overcome the evils of poverty, injustice, and discrimination. In a universe of unlimited material resources, economic growth together with a renewed commitment to equality and justice can provide a good life for all mankind.

Ethics for a World of Limited Resources

But now, in 2005, there are 6.3 billion people living on Earth, and the human population is still growing by about 200,000 extra people every day. It may well exceed 9 billion by midcentury. The Earth has little virgin land and few untapped natural resources that remain to be exploited. When new fuel and mineral resources are discovered, they lie deep underground, far beneath the oceans, or high in the Arctic. They also occur in smaller fields and in lower concentrations. More human effort and more energy is needed to extract them and to transport them to where they are to be used. Petroleum is a case in point. It takes more human effort and more energy to discover new oil fields, and more equipment and more energy to transport the newly found oil to where it is needed. The net energy gained decreases and its cost rises.[4]

In addition, nearly half of the people on Earth now crowd into megacities. There, all foods need to be imported, complex water and sewage systems must be built and maintained, and all trash and wastes trucked out. Ever more energy and ever more human effort is required just to provide these vital necessities—services that nature once provided almost without cost when people led decentralized and nearly self-sufficient agricultural ways of life.

In short, the physical demands of modern life and those of the expanding urban population work together to necessitate a steady increase in the need for more land, food, water, fuel, and natural resources. An exponential increase in the exploitation of physical or biological resources will eventually deplete any finite reserves. Even now, the quantity available per person is steadily decreasing. When scarcity becomes inexorable, the ethical and economic systems that are dedicated to continual growth will not have the physical resources necessary to continue to function. They will simply collapse.

An ethics for a finite world cannot be one that promotes or even allows continual growth either in the human population or in the production of material goods and services.

The Factually Necessary Condition for Western Ethics

The conditional nature of the egalitarian and human-centered ethics, which the Western nations proclaim unreservedly, can easily be demonstrated. One has only to examine the logical consequences of the hypothesis that an intractable scarcity has arisen. An unconditional loyalty to the principle of equal justice for all requires a rationing of scarce necessities. A strict allocation is required to assure that everyone shares the hardship equally. But the rationing must become more and more severe as the scarcity gets more intractable—especially if the population continues to grow and/or the economy continues to expand. The asymptote toward which this process is directed is a condition where more and more people have less and less, until the lives of all are degraded and starvation becomes the lot of everyone.

Such a societal demise, however, is justified only by valid reasoning from totally unrealistic premises; it could never happen. The reasoning in support of this claim can hardly be faulted. Under conditions of an intractable scarcity, competition is inevitable. The lack of vital resources causes people to starve and the economic system to crash. All who remain resolutely loyal to the universal principles of moral equality and equal justice simply die out. By contrast, those driven by an instinct to survive break ranks; they just stop living by egalitarian principles. They use the same logic that governs the game of musical chairs: if there are more people than chairs, then some players will be left standing when the music stops. Those left standing are no longer players. The ones who struggle most to get a seat continue playing. Similarly, people who dedicate their lives to the universal principles of equality and justice are no longer players in the game of life. Having sacrificed everything for moral principles, they simply die out. The players who are aggressive, competitive, and endowed with an instinct to survive continue to play the game. The game they play, however, will be a different one. It will be played by a different set of moral rules.

This simple thought experiment proves that the egalitarian ethics that the Western nations proclaim and enforce cannot be universal; it cannot be applied equally to all mankind under all circumstances. If the physical sources exist to be shared equally and fairly with everyone, people can live by this ethics. If an overpopulated world with a deteriorating environment has a scarcity of land and physical resources, for everyone to live by this ethics becomes physically impossible. In short, an abundance of land and natural resources is a necessary condition for people to live by the Western principles of universal human rights and equal justice for all.

The Failure to Recognize the Contingent Nature of Moral Knowledge

If ever a persisting and intractable shortage of land, energy, water, or natural resources should arise, the ethics that survive will be ones that build on the environmental principle—the obligation to preserve the durability and integrity of the Earth's biosystem. An ethics suited to a finite world will be an environmental ethics. Its moral rules will be flexible—context-dependent rather than universal, egalitarian, and unconditional. Indeed, the rules for moral life must change with the variations in population densities and with the changing support capacities of the environments that provide the physical resources necessary for moral life. As the density of populations changes, and as the support capacity of environments evolves, this ethics will use empirical evidence—not a priori arguments—to justify the human rights and freedoms, as well as moral duties, that are physically possible in finite environments.

The error of Western ethics is that it attempts to justify moral laws and principles by well-reasoned arguments from a human-centered definition of moral status and from moral principles that are merely assumed. So conceived, moral judgments are categorical in their certainty and universal in their scope. In effect, the a priori, rationalist method of Western ethics makes human genes rather than human activities determine moral rights and humanitarian duties. As a consequence, the rationalist method makes it impossible for a factual state of affairs—such as scarcity or overpopulation—to limit or refute its moral claims. It cannot take account of the contingent nature of moral behavior—that factual circumstances can cause behavior that once was moral to become immoral. Thus, Western ethics, in principle, cannot prevent overpopulation and environmental breakdown from annulling the purpose of moral life.

By contrast, an ethics suited to a finite world builds on the environmental principle. It recognizes the conditional character of moral behavior. To be sure, this principle need not apply when people live in areas of vast, open lands and untapped natural resources. But it must apply and must be enforced when an excessive population or an excessive demand for material goods and services threatens to overwhelm the biological commons and, thereby, makes moral life physically impossible.

Two facts about life in a finite world have great moral significance. One is that conditions of impending scarcity cause all unnecessary and excessive births to become immoral. The other is that conditions of scarcity render immoral any further destructive exploitation of material resources. Only when nature is able to sustain human material demands can human rights and equal justice be possible for all mankind. The possibility of scarcity makes the obligation stand clear: moral behavior can never allow scarcity to nullify moral ideals and principles.

Summary

All the principles fundamental to Western ethics are human-centered. They originated when land and resources seemed unlimited. In such a world, the moral principles that people in the Western nations commonly take for granted clearly furthered human survival. They allowed societies to flourish and to take over more of the Earth's land and biological resources. In a dynamic and evolving world, however, what worked in the past may not work in the future. Human success has now become the cause of human woes. By eliminating the competition from other living things—the larger animals, the diseased organisms, the forests, grasslands, weeds, and pests—all the natural constraints imposed by the competition of other organisms are disappearing. Nothing but a species-imposed constraint remains to prevent human activity from causing the biosystem to break down. This constraint can be stated as the environmental principle: the well-being of the environment must have moral precedence over the needs and interests of mankind. The human-centered principles of Western ethics cannot be universal and unqualified. In a finite world, ethical theories must be dependent on the ability of an enduring and resilient biosystem to sustain them. A finite Earth makes all moral theories conditional.

Rationalism in Ethics

The rationalism of Western ethics is revealed in its assumption that reason and the coherence of our considered and unbiased moral judgments can justify moral laws and principles. These nonempirical criteria, however, give moral conclusions a certainty that factual information can neither limit nor refute. Because moral theories change the course of events in nature, any human activity that uses matter or energy—even behavior validly entailed by moral theory—can cause unforeseen factual consequences. Inevitably, ethical theories must pass factual tests: they are tenable if their practice causes much benefit and an acceptable amount of harm. They are absurd if their practice causes enough harm to overwhelm all benefit.

The fact that the moral behavior that moral theory validly entails can cause hardship and even moral tragedy refutes the rationalist methodological hypothesis that reason and valid arguments are the criteria that can justify an ethical theory.

What Is Rationalism in Ethics?

Rationalism in ethics is the methodological hypothesis that reason and the coherence of our considered judgments over a whole range of moral issues are the sources of moral knowledge. But people constantly forget that reason and the coherence of beliefs provide no new information; all they can do is restate what is already given in the grammar, definitions, and premises assumed. Thus, as long as moral theories remain in the a priori domain of definition and assumption, moral conclusions can, indeed, be valid and self-evident; they can be universally and unconditionally true. But their truth in the a priori domain does not give them any reference or any relevance to events in the physical world.

Without examination—indeed, without even an awareness of the speculative nature of the hypothesis—people in the Western world generally believe that ethics concerns only what ought to be and not what actually happens. They consider moral knowledge to be a higher form of truth that stands above the contingent knowledge of things and events in nature. Furthermore, by appeals to such nonempirical criteria as reason, intuition, the logic of moral language, the demands of equal justice, the still-small voice of childhood conditioning, and/or the word of God, the conviction is unquestioned that knowledge of ethics is authoritative and unchanging. In short, rationalism in ethics fosters the illusion that reason and valid arguments give moral laws and principles a certainty and universal authority that scientific laws and principles can never attain.

Because ethical rationalism gives ethics a nonempirical origin, moral claims and counterclaims are argued out in human hearts and minds. There they are held to be verified when validly reasoned moral conclusions from moral theory agree with commonly accepted moral principles and a human-centered definition of value. But the validity of conclusions in the a priori domain of definition and assumption cannot give them any relevance to events in nature. Ethical arguments and counterarguments can go on and on as different definitions of value and different moral assumptions are shown to entail contrasting moral judgments. Safely ensconced in the abstract domain of a priori thought, where objective factual evidence cannot refute their moral theories, professionals in moral philosophy are rewarded with tenure and promotion when they play the circular ethical game of argument and counterargument.

It is mere hubris, however, to assume that human reason can devise a theory of ethics or justice that is capable of directing events in the physical world. It is also an illusion to believe that when reason makes seemingly unbiased moral judgments coherent, it provides mankind with knowledge of the correct moral behavior for all cultures and all environments. So conceived and so justified, the moral authority of ethics is final. To be faithful to moral principles no matter what the consequences may be is commonly taken to be a sign of the highest moral character. By placing moral theory in the domain of nonempirical knowledge, rationalism in ethics makes it impossible in principle for factual data ever to refute an ethics or theory of justice. Thus, the rationalist method disconnects ethics from the changing needs of life in a biological order that was created and is maintained by the mutual support of its members. It disconnects moral behavior from the physical constraints of a finite world.

The Logical Form
of the Refutation of Rationalism in Ethics
Premise one: the theory of rationalism in ethics entails that the knowledge of ethics can be universal and certain. Premise two: all human activity in the physical world causes a tangled skein of benefit and harm. It is possible that an ethical theory can require moral behavior that causes a society

to die out or environments to collapse. If so, that theory is self-negating and absurd. It is false that the knowledge of ethics can be universal and certain.

Conclusion: the theory of rationalism in ethics is mistaken.

Some may find fault with this refutation because they believe premise two to be incorrect. The problem of trying to justify the truistic claim that moral behavior changes the course of events in nature is baffling. Can any moral philosopher or any religious zealot deny it? To do so would trivialize moral beliefs and make moral behavior irrelevant to life on Earth. Does anyone doubt that human activities sometimes cause unexpected and even disastrous results? Doesn't the absurdity of its denial prove it to be a moral axiom that no ethics can be practiced in a finite world when to practice it causes it to be physically impossible to practice it?

Every ethics commands people to modify their behavior and thereby to change what happens in the world. Implicit in this claim is the prediction that society or mankind will benefit. But this factual prediction can be false: the moral behavior required by a moral theory can cause actual harm, or even moral disaster. The fact that any ethical theory can fail empirical tests demonstrates that moral knowledge never is universal and certain. It demonstrates the error of rationalist method in ethics.

The Contingent Consequences
Caused by Enforcing the Principles of Western Ethics
If the principles of an ethical theory are universal, they must be enforced without favoritism or discrimination. That enforcement, however, can cause contingent consequences. It can produce benefit in one environment and yet produce

great suffering and even moral tragedy in another. The following examples illustrate the fact that empirical evidence—not reason and valid arguments—can prove the error of a moral theory.

When a small number of farmers clear forestland to make farms, they can produce food for themselves and sell the excess to city residents. When, however, millions of poor people clear all the forestland in their nation, they cause soil erosion, the destruction of the ecosystems, and global fluctuations of floods and droughts. They cause the environment to break down and bring tragedy to all. Thus, different environmental circumstances change the act of clearing land for a farm to feed your family from being moral to being immoral.

When the number of fishermen is small, to fish benefits both fishermen and consumers who do not fish. But when vast numbers of fishermen use high-tech fleets to scour the oceans, fish stocks crash and fishing stops. In a growing population, to follow the principle that everyone has the right to earn a living by fishing causes harm to overwhelm the benefit. Different environmental circumstances change fishing from being moral to being immoral.

In a country having vast, open lands and untapped resources, the birth of a child can be a blessed event. But in regions where a dense population and its excessive physical demands have devastated the environment, it becomes a tragedy. It only increases the scarcity of land, food, water, and the possibility for employment; it causes parents to sell their children into prostitution or indentured labor. The birth of extra children can destabilize any society that tries to support a growing population in a degraded environment; it only exacerbates human suffering. Different environmental circumstances change the birth of a child from being a blessed and moral event to being immoral.

When a vast amount of petroleum remains to be discovered and exploited, to use it for transportation, for fueling electric plants, for home heating, for mechanized agriculture, and for manufacturing and running industrial equipment saves human labor and rapidly increases supply of food and consumer goods. It allows great numbers of people to have a high standard of living. But if the Earth's limited stock of petroleum begins to run out and the price of fuel rises dramatically, or if the carbon dioxide that results from burning it begins to destabilize the world's atmosphere, then the use of petroleum to power the production of material goods and services must be drastically curtailed, or even eliminated. If some equally dense, environmentally benign, and low-cost source of new energy is not immediately found, then growth-oriented moral and economic systems break down. The human population and the expanding global economic system simply crash, just as an algal bloom ends in an algal bust. The lack of cheap fuel could eventually end all economic activity that is dedicated to a perpetual increase in production. In effect, different environmental circumstances change the burning of fossil fuel from being moral to being immoral.

The present system of corporate capitalism together with global free trade allows wealth and power to be concentrated in an ever-smaller elite, while the vast majority of the world's people have lives degraded by crowding and poverty. If the present capitalist system should cause such a contrast of wealth and power, it would thwart the second goal of ethics. A new social and economic experiment would be needed. Perhaps a modern replica of the French

Revolution will be the means by which a new order can be established. Or possibly, and surely preferably, a peaceful and democratic means may be found to initiate a new social-economic experiment. In any case, it is not reason and valid arguments that justify different social-economic orders. Rather, it is the laws and limits of nature that determine which ethical systems will work and which will not work. The slow and faltering process of trial and error is method for discovering the moral theory that better fulfills the environmental and human goals of ethics.

The Logical Origin of Rationalism in Ethics

For every logical class, there is a set of properties that defines the class. These essential properties characterize every member. All the other properties of individuals are accidental or nonessential; they may characterize some members and not others.

As previously noted, rationalism in ethics is a methodological assumption that maintains that reason and valid arguments can yield knowledge of ethics. To be sure, if all human beings were the same as peas in a pod, they would all have the same morally relevant properties and would act identically under all circumstances. Then it would be self-evident, as the rationalist method in ethics assumes, that moral laws and principles apply universally to all mankind.

As a case in point, if one defines the Moon, as Aristotle did, to be a heavenly body made of incorruptible, changeless, and immaterial matter, it would be valid and self-evidently true that the Moon is eternal. But the self-evidence of this conclusion does not allow that conclusion to override empirical knowledge of the Moon's chemical and physical properties; it does not make the Moon, in fact, eternal.

Similarly, if the defining properties of the human species include moral equality, then it is self-evident that human rights, humanitarian obligations, personal freedoms, and the prospects for personal fulfillment are the same for all mankind. But the self-evidence of these moral claims holds only in the domain of definition and conjecture. Their truth in this abstract domain of definition and valid reasoning can neither cause unequal people to be equal nor make them produce equal consequences.

The following are examples of cases in which the accidental characteristics of human beings are the major determinants of what happens in the physical world. The fact that human individuals differ so profoundly in their accidental or nondefining characteristics makes it hard even to imagine what the concept of moral equality could possibly mean.

The various stages of life cause human beings to differ fundamentally. The fetus, the newborn, the child, the teenager, the parents, and the aged are all members of the human race. The accidental differences between these human individuals cause them to do and to want different things. Their different abilities, functions, duties, stages in life, and life expectancies cause their rights, liberties, functions, and moral responsibilities to differ—to be unequal. To treat all these individuals as if they were equal when, in fact, they are grossly unequal is absurd. It can cause hardship, even disaster.

Different cultures cause citizens to have different goals in life, to hold different conceptions of human welfare, and to want different things both for themselves and for their children. Some people want to kill all abortion providers as murderers, while others defend a woman's right to control her own body and to have an abortion on demand. Some want defective infants to be allowed to die at birth, while others want them to be kept alive at public expense for the rest of their lives. Some believe that all knowledge is given by faith, while others believe that all knowledge is justified by either mathematics and logic or by factual evidence. Some want children to be educated in the teachings of the Bible or the Koran as the source of knowledge; others want them to be educated in modern, democratic humanism and global, free-market capitalism. These accidental cultural differences cause a chaotic complex of consequences.

In what sense can the principle of the moral equality give all people from all cultures equal human rights, equal moral obligations, and equal prospects for their welfare? Isn't it absurd to allow the valid deductions from a moral theory of human equality and equal justice to defy all factual evidence? Can anyone advocate an ethics that causes hardship, and even disaster, to overwhelm all benefit?[5]

It is an undeniable fact that environmental differences determine the factual consequences caused by moral behavior. People suffer when they have trashed their environments, or when they have more children than they can care for. An egalitarian ethics, however, is commonly understood to require mankind to provide every human being with equal access to the necessities of life. To be sure, such aid does relieve immediate human misery, but it does nothing to change the behavior that caused the need in the first place. Human misery is not the same as a hole in the roof that can be repaired and stay fixed. Rather, human misery is the result of a process—a series of causes. If it is relieved for the moment, the same causes only make misery and need recur. Doesn't factual evidence demonstrate that reason and valid arguments are faulty criteria for justifying an ethics or a theory of justice? If to live by the rules of an ethical theory causes tragic consequences, no other assessment is possible than that the ethical theory is not viable; it cannot be a guide for human affairs. It needs to be discarded, or at least revised and tested again.

When the principle of human equality assures everybody of the human right to food, water, medical care, shelter, and employment, this right nullifies the responsibility of both individuals and nations for their own welfare. To implement these rights subsidizes the status quo of a growth in population and of an expansion in environmental exploitation. In effect, fostering overpopulation and environmental degradation increases human suffering. If an ethics causes tragic consequences for the individual, the society, or the environment, this fact is objective evidence of the error of the methodology and the ethical theory that caused the disaster.

To enforce the ideal of moral equality has two side effects. Both make the goals of moral life impossible to attain.

One side effect of assuring that everyone's vital needs are met is that the individuals who can generate need are rewarded, while all those who give aid are penalized by depriving them of their property. The fact is that ignorant and irresponsible people can harm themselves and cause their own misery. For instance, they can have many children whom they cannot support; they can abuse their bodies and their health; they can destroy their environments. In short, they cause the suffering and hardship that others must relieve. But the relief givers can do nothing to control the causes of these ills. Inevitably, unconditional aid causes dire consequences. It subsidizes all increases in population wherever they may occur. It also increases the human demands on the Earth's limited lands and resources. Yet, at the same time, it forces aid givers to diminish their own resources and possibly limit the number of their own children. In nature one tends to get what one rewards and not to get what one punishes. Indeed, no ethical theory can endure if the moral behavior that it demands prevents it from attaining its moral goals.

The other side effect is that when people are not allowed to experience the painful or destructive consequences of their own behavior, all the natural controls are removed by which individuals and societies learn to correct their mistakes. In effect, the ethics of universal human rights and equal welfare of all human beings makes mankind—not individuals—responsible for the health and well-being of *all* individuals. It is unlikely that any ethics can succeed if it separates moral obligation from moral responsibility—that is, if it tries to make moral obligations replace the biological controls by which nature maintains the intrinsic fitness of the individual and the species.

The rationalist method in ethics gives rise to the belief that human reason and human sensibilities can generate the laws and principles of ethics. This method of justifying an ethical theory, however, is just another instance of human hubris; it fosters the arrogant belief that human beings can establish the order of events in the physical world. It also fosters the species-flattering belief that an ethics that sometimes promotes human welfare under some circumstances can never cause harm, can never cause a society to die out or an environment to break down. When the principle of human moral equality is taken to be a priori certain, it makes a factual prediction. It predicts that when everyone has an equal education and equal opportunities, the equal welfare of all mankind will be realized. This prediction errs on two counts.

First, these equality principles fail because they can provide equal results only if the individuals are equal to begin with. If incompetent individuals have an equal opportunity to compete with the competent, the equality of opportunity only guarantees that the competent will win and the incompetent will lose.

Second, if necessary resources should ever become inadequate to provide everyone with vital necessities, equal opportunity cannot create more resources out of nothing. Intractable scarcity causes it to be physically impossible to give all human beings an adequate ration of what they need to live. Scarcity makes it physically impossible to implement the ideal of moral equality. Scarcity also makes it impossible to use egalitarian principles and universal human rights to determine who or what will be allotted the necessities of life and who or what will have to do without them.

Further defects in the rationalist method and in the egalitarian principle that it supposedly justifies are worth noting.

When confronted by the fact that billions of people in Africa, South America, and Asia lack the human rights as well as the economic and educational opportunities that the people of the industrialized nations enjoy, the principles of Western ethics call for more food, more medical care, more hospitals, more schools, more roads and infrastructure, more municipal water and sewage-treatment plants, more refuse collection, more agricultural development, more trade and business expansion, more jobs, more parks and libraries, and on, and on. The pragmatic effect of such demands is to cause a steady increase in the human exploitation of the world's land and natural resources. Western ethics founded on equal justice and an anthropocentric definition of value fails because it has no principles that can impose moral constraints that reduce the size of the human population and that limit the human exploitation of the world environment.

Again, because the rationalist method allows mere membership in the human race to justify universal human rights and humanitarian obligations, these rights and obligations cannot be diminished or annulled by the accidental or nondefining characteristics of human beings. Thereby, the rationalist method founds ethics on a false assessment of fact. It falsely assumes that the principles of moral equality and universal human rights can nullify the causal effects of the accidental characteristics of genetic endowment, age, reproductive behavior, culture, climate, and environmental health. To be specific, it falsely assumes that moral fiat can make the fetus as intelligent and self-sustaining as the mother, the aged as vigorous and productive as the young, and those who choose instant gratification as healthy as those who restrain the immediate satisfaction of desires in favor of their own long-term welfare. In effect, it denies that different accidental properties of human beings change what happens to them, to society, and to the environment.

In short, the rationalist methodology in ethics has the relation of cause and effect exactly backward. The human equality postulated by Western moral theory does not overcome the physical consequences caused by accidental human differences between human beings. Rather, the accidental differences determine the human rights and duties that are possible for them to have in the finite environments in which they live.

A Summary of the Errors of Rationalism in Ethics

The accidental differences between human beings make people want different things and make them work for different goals. These differences determine what people do and what happens to them. They establish prospects people have for satisfying their needs, for their personal fulfillment, and for the welfare of society and the environment. The nonessential characteristics of different human individuals make it physically impossible for them all to have the same rights, duties, freedoms, opportunities, and prospects for a satisfying life.

When moral theories are justified by rational arguments within the a priori domain of definition and assumption, theories can make no empirical claims. In this domain, valid moral conclusions may have no relevance to the needs of life in a biosystem created and sustained by the mutual support of its organisms. Only hardship or disaster result when all people are treated as if they were equal—both morally equal and equal in what they produce—when, in fact, these assumptions are false.

The status quo is only reinforced when all human beings have to do to get more humanitarian aid is to increase their need. They can continue to have high reproductive rates, to devastate their local environments, to abuse their bodies and their health, and to maintain their religion and their customs. The pragmatic effect is only to increase human numbers and intensify human need.

An analogy commonly used by environmentalists is apropos: the rationalist method of justifying ethics makes it like a car engineered to have a bigger engine with more power and acceleration but no breaks. It is an ethics designed for disaster.

Reason and the Rule of Law

Henri Bergson is one of the few philosophers who recognized the limits of rational thought. Reason, or intellect, can function only when the concepts it uses in thinking have clear-cut definitions and when they and the objects they refer to remain constant through time. It evolved as a tool that enables human beings to use experienced regularities to predict future events and, thereby, improve the prospects for their survival.[6] It is not a uniquely human and possibly divine faculty that provides final knowledge of the fundamental principles of ethics.

People brought up in the rationalist tradition of Western ethics simply take it for granted that ethics is founded on the rule of law. They fail to take account of the factual condition that must be met before the rule of law is possible. It is that all individuals subsumed under the law can be treated as if they were interchangeable variables in the statement of the law. When this condition is not met, the rule of law can cause a quagmire of contradictory consequences.

The government of the United States was founded on the proposition that all men—all citizens—are equal. This supposed self-evident truth entails such important propositions as all citizens are equal before the law; all have the right to life, liberty, and the pursuit of happiness and an equal opportunity to realize these goals.

The empirical evidence is clear: legislatures can pass laws that can be validly deduced from the principles of equality and equal justice. It is just as clear that they can pass other laws that contradict these constitutional principles.

First, some examples are given of legislation that can be validly inferred from the constitutional principle of human equality:

- Discrimination is illegal because laws that give special privileges to some or inflict hardship on others fail to treat all citizens equally. Thus, laws have been enacted that make it illegal to discriminate between people on the basis of race, religion, sex, age, physical handicap, mental deficiency, or health.

- Once the assumption that all citizens are equal is taken for granted, the fact that some people lack food, housing, employment, and medical care proves that discrimination or injustice has occurred. Accordingly, legislation has been enacted to provide food stamps, low-cost housing, unemployment compensation, medical care, and old-age assistance to those in need. It is supposed to assure that all citizens have equal access to the necessities of life.

- Again, the principle that all citizens are equal allows the valid conclusion to be drawn that if the income of the average woman is lower than that of the average man, all citizens are not treated equally; sexual discrimination has occurred. Hence, special laws have been enacted to enforce equal employment, equal opportunities, equal wages, and equal prospects for advancement for both men and women.

- Again, the constitutional principles of human equality give equal rights to all who are physically

disabled. Legislation has been passed that guarantees the right of the handicapped to have equal
access to public buildings, public toilets, and businesses open to the public. Although some laws
have been proposed, none have been enacted to
put paved paths or cable cars through wilderness
areas and national parks. The handicapped still
face discrimination: they do not yet have the same
access as other citizens to all public lands.

• Finally, it takes little logical acuity for President
Bush to deduce from the principle of human
equality that fetuses in the United States have the
equal right of all U.S. citizens to life and to be pro-
tected from murder. Therefore, he calls for legislation to prohibit all abortions.

Just as clearly, other laws have been enacted that contradict the principles of equal justice and the equality of all
citizens before the law:

• Despite the fact that all sexual discrimination violates the constitutional principle of equality and is
illegal, strict sexual discrimination occurs in
sports, marriage, military service, swimwear, and
the use of public toilets. Such discrimination is
either enforced by law or simply accepted. Women
cannot play on professional football teams.
Genetic tests separate men's from women's teams
in all Olympic sports. Fines prevent women from
wearing topless swimsuits. It is a misdemeanor
for men to use women's toilets. No women have to

register for the draft. The laws of most states discriminate against citizens solely on the ground of gender when they forbid the marriage of couples of the same sex.

• When human equality is taken for granted, factual differences between racial groups are proof that racial discrimination has occurred. To be specific, the fact that black citizens earn less on average than white citizens proves that they suffer discrimination. Again, facts prove discrimination when the percentage of black students who graduate from institutions of higher learning is less than their percentage in the general population. In order to compensate for the past abuses, affirmative-action legislation has been enacted. It gives preference in job opportunities and in admittance to universities to a group of citizens who have had a long history of humiliating abuse. In effect, these laws give favored treatment to some citizens and penalize others solely on the grounds of their race. Affirmative action is legislation that enforces racial discrimination.

• Although all U.S. citizens are guaranteed equal rights, still legislatures—all of whose members are over twenty-one years of age—have passed laws that allow one group of voting citizens to discriminate against another group of voting citizens. Laws allow citizens who are over twenty-one to deprive citizens who are under twenty-one of the right to drink alcoholic beverages. Such laws clearly violate the constitutional principle that all U.S. citizens have equal rights under the law.

- Congress has passed laws that force men who reach the age of eighteen to register for military service. Registration for the draft does not apply to women or older men; these privileged citizens have no legal obligation to register. By applying only to men who have reached eighteen years of age, the law clearly contradicts the principle of the equality of all citizens before the law.

- Finally, the principle that all citizens have equal rights and obligations seems to require all citizens to pay an equal tax. Instead, the government has recognized that U.S. citizens are not equal in that they have different incomes and different abilities to pay. Accordingly, the government has changed the law. Now the tax law states that only people within certain income categories are equal and have to pay equal taxes. In effect, the accidental property of income has been made a defining property of a set of subclasses of citizens who, by definition, have approximately the same income and, therefore, the same tax liability.

Indeed, present U.S. tax laws build on the principle that citizens are unequal. They rank all citizens according to income categories. Those in high-income brackets pay high-income taxes; those in low-income brackets pay little or no tax. Furthermore, the tax laws give a tax advantage to people who own or inherit immense wealth. The favored few who have fortunes in stocks, bonds, and real estate pay no federal tax at all on their wealth as long as they do not sell any investments for cash.

Obviously, the Internal Revenue Service (IRS) discriminates against some U.S. citizens, while it gives great advantages to others. Can anyone figure out how to deduce this hodge-podge of tax laws from the constitutional principles of human equality and their equality before the law? Isn't it clear that the U.S. tax laws are merely expedient ploys that the government uses to raise the funds it needs? Doesn't the government use laws to discriminate against any citizens it wishes?

Something is wrong! The rule of law is not the fundamental principle of ethics. Rather, it can direct human affairs only when laws produce results that further the moral goals. Whenever the rule of law causes undue hardship or destabilizes society, it is simply disregarded. In effect, the error of the rationalist methodology for ethics is to be found in its empirically absurd assumption that the rule of law is the fundamental principle of ethics.

The rationalist method in ethics errs in its assumption that reason and valid arguments can generate the moral laws and principles that cause changes in the course of events in nature. It errs because it has the causal order backward. The laws and limits of nature determine both what happens and what can happen. Nature determines when sufficient regularities exist to allow moral laws and principles to be enforced, and when the lack of regularities makes it absurd or disastrous to enforce the rule of law.

The inconsistencies that are noted above regarding the enforcement and disregard of the rule of law have their origin in the diversity of citizens' accidental properties: their wealth, income, intelligence, education, physical ability, interests, age, and ways of life. Although these accidental properties are not essential to the definition of the human being, they still cause a chaotic diversity of outcomes in what people have, in how society is organized, and in what environmental stability is possible. Such diversity makes it physically impossible in principle to treat all citizens equally when they are not. It cannot give them all equal rights and freedoms regardless of their age, health, and abilities, regardless of what they do.

The fact is that the laws of moral behavior can cause much benefit and little harm when they govern the moral behavior of people who are essentially similar and who act in situations that are the same for all practical purposes. But the same laws can cause harm, or even tragedy, when they are enforced on people, societies, or environments that differ profoundly in their accidental properties. Thus, laws are constantly revised, discarded, or forgotten whenever their enforcement causes significant personal injury, breaks established social conventions, or damages the environment. The consequences caused by the enforcement of laws can never be known by a priori thought. Hence, the rule of law cannot be known to cause benefit rather than hardship or tragedy.

Empirical evidence shows that whimsy—or at least expediency—allows governments and societies to make laws that allow them to get what they desire, at least for the moment. The chaotic inconsistency with which laws are enacted and enforced is evidence of the defects in the concept of their universal application. The rule of law always threatens to become the tyranny of law.

Interpretation as Confirmation

When an arbitrary definition or assumed concept is used to describe perceived objects or events, it begs the question to take statements that are built on such reference as proof that the definition or concept is correct. This circularity occurs when actual noises that are heard in the night are taken to prove that ghosts exist. It occurs again when an unexpected recovery from a usually fatal disease is interpreted as proof of the existence of a benevolent God. Again, a similar self-deception allowed the phlogiston chemists of old to see the upward motion of flames as proof that elemental fire seeks its natural place in the heavens. To interpret sensory experience is not empirical proof that the statements that result are true.

A similar circularity occurs in classical utilitarian ethics when the goal of ethics is defined as maximizing happiness for the greatest number of people. This utilitarian definition, however, merely stipulates the criteria for making universal moral judgments. But it is entirely arbitrary to use a moral definition to describe real things and then take the resulting description of them as factual proof that the arbitrary definition is correct. Anyone who accepts such circular thinking can go about the seemingly moral task of directing human behavior so as to bring about the utilitarian goal of maximizing human happiness and human numbers. This factual task, however, is still as specious as the original definition on which it is grounded.

A utilitarian definition of the goal of ethics is just as gratuitous and arbitrary as one that would define the aesthetic goal of a painting to be to maximize the total area of red pigment in the painting: the greater the percentage of the area that is red, the greater the artistic merit. Indeed, it is possible to rank all works of art according to the percentage of area of red pigment in the painting. The aesthetic assessment that would result, however, is absurd; it is just as whimsical and capricious as the original definition.

Moral philosophers who think that moral knowledge falls in the domain of nonempirical certainty use a similar circularity. They invent a moral theory whose laws and principles logically entail the dos and don'ts that accord with the coherent judgments of the moral traditions of the society. They apply their theory to actual cases. Then they interpret the fact that the moral behavior, which their theory logically entails, agrees with actual moral practice as if it were factual evidence of their theory's correctness. To repeat, it begs the question to use an arbitrary factual reference to construct statements and then take the statements to be proof that the reference is correct. Factual reference is not justification. Interpretation is not confirmation.

Summary

All living things, including all human beings, are dependent on the ability of the Earth's biosystem to support them. By trying to justify moral behavior on a priori—nonempirical—grounds, the rationalist paradigm causes moral philosophers to ignore the factual origins of human life and the factual dependence of an ethical theory on the ability of the Earth's finite resources to support the way of life that it proposes.

To date, the Western system of ethics has withstood the test of time. Without doubt, however, countless other ethical systems have failed when the people who tried to live by the rules of their faulty ethics simply died out. Inevitably, a necessary condition for moral life exists. Namely, that ample lands and material resources be available for human use.

Any moral theory must be rejected if to live as it requires repudiates the environmental principle. Inevitably, the existence of a necessary factual condition for moral life proves that reason and valid arguments alone never suffice to justify a moral theory. It demonstrates the falsity of the rationalist paradigm in ethics.

The profound mistake of ethical rationalism can be emphasized. Ethical rationalism makes believe that valid inferences from an anthropocentric definition of value and anthropocentric moral principles that are merely assumed can justify the principles of equal justice, universal human rights, and humanitarian duties. So conceived and so justified, moral behavior disregards the dependence of moral life on the ability of an enduring and resilient environment to sustain that behavior. If an ethical theory causes the demise of societies that try to live by it, that ethics is self-repudiating. It must be revised or discarded. It is mistaken; it is wrong.

The Fallacy of the Naturalistic Fallacy

The naturalistic fallacy is commonly stated to be the mistake of trying to derive the *ought* from the *is*. It is the supposed failure to recognize that ethical statements differ in kind from factual statements.

The naturalistic fallacy, however, is misconceived. It builds on the hypothesis that ethics falls in the domain of nonempirical knowledge. But this hypothesis cannot be correct. The purpose of ethics is to require behavior that changes the course of events in nature. Knowledge of what happens or cannot happen in the world clearly is empirical knowledge. Furthermore, it is possible for the behavior mandated by a moral theory to cause actual benefit or actual harm; it can even cause a society to die out, or an environment that once supported it to collapse. In such cases, the ethical theory is not viable; it becomes extinct along with the society that tried to live by it. Because empirical evidence can nullify an ethical theory, knowledge of ethics is contingent. The fact that there is no conceptual gulf that separates the *ought* from the *is* demonstrates the fallacy of the naturalistic fallacy.

Earthbound, edited by Tom Regan, includes an article by Kristin Shrader-Frechette. In it she writes that the naturalistic fallacy "consists in the failure to recognize that *ethical* statements are different in kind from *nonethical* ones. It is committed whenever one attempts to define ethical characteristics (e.g., what is morally desirable) in nonethical terms (e.g., what people actually desire)."[7] This clear, simple statement called my attention again to a long-standing conviction that the claim of the naturalistic fallacy in ethics is misconceived, that the naturalistic fallacy is itself a fallacy.

The naturalistic fallacy ethicists (NFE) correctly note that ethical statements differ from simple factual statements about people's needs and interests. They also correctly note that the moral conventions of society differ essentially from behavior that is morally justified. But such differences do not entail that knowledge of ethics is "different in kind from nonethical" knowledge. They do not make moral knowledge different in kind from all knowledge that has an empirical warrant.

Although much has been written in criticism, the fact remains that professional moral philosophers still take it for granted that there is a naturalistic fallacy in ethics. As the fallacy is commonly stated, it is said to be impossible to derive the *ought* from the *is*. This sweeping generalization, however, has to be false. If the *ought* is not derived from the *is*, what else, pray tell, is there for the *ought* to be derived from? Can it come from nothing? Can it come from what does not exist? Isn't the naturalistic fallacy grounded in a fundamental absurdity?

The need remains to examine this supposed fallacy. The following arguments and discussions demonstrate that the naturalistic fallacy is misconceived. Perhaps this supposed fallacy can finally be laid to a well-deserved eternal rest.

The Circularity of the Assumption That a Gulf Separates Values from Facts

Many contemporary moral philosophers use the techniques of logical analysis to show that the fundamental principles of ethics are implicit in the logic of moral language. They fail to note, however, that their arguments are circular. If the analysis of moral language shows that normative and value statements are distinct in kind from factual ones, then that distinction is already inherent in the definitions of the moral words of that language. Analysis can only unpack information that is implicit in the definitions and assumptions of the language. It cannot generate new knowledge, especially knowledge of the contingent consequences caused by population growth, irresponsible procreation, pollution, economic expansion, or environmental breakdown. Linguistic analysis cannot prove that moral language entails knowledge of the contingent behavior that supports the evolving needs of life or that conforms to the laws and limits of nature. In short, analysis cannot prove that the behavior required by moral language has anything to do with life on this finite Earth.

Dual Domains of Value and Fact

The criteria that the NFE use to justify moral statements create a conceptual gulf that separates the domain of ethical knowledge from that of empirical knowledge. The NFE assumed that empirical statements are either true or false. By contrast, ethical statements are not true or false, only valid or invalid, right or wrong. The two different domains of knowledge require that statements be classified as to their type of discourse before they can be justified. Factual knowledge is warranted by experiment and empirical evidence. On the other hand, moral knowledge according to the NFE has no factual warrant. Rather, it is warranted only by valid arguments that demonstrate the coherence of the human-centered and egalitarian principles of the Western world. The distinction in the method for justifying moral knowledge perpetuates belief in a conceptual gulf that separates the domain of the knowledge of ethics from the domain of empirical knowledge.

Because the NFE use nonempirical and human-centered criteria to justify their ethical theories, they are ensconced in the rationalist tradition of Western ethics. They appeal to reason, conscience, the logic of moral language, the coherence of considered moral judgments over a range of questions, the rule of law, and the demands of equal justice to justify moral principles, universal human rights, and humanitarian duties. In this thought-world of definition and self-evident truth, ethical theories of equality and justice can meld with all forms of speculation. Thought-lions can lie down and live in peace with thought-lambs.

Such theories, however, need have nothing to do with life in nature, where lions have evolved together with lambs and where both species would be impaired if live lions did not eat live lambs. In a thought-world, moral laws and human rights can be universal in scope, and philanthropic obligations can be unconditional in their application. But the logical properties that define the agents and the laws of moral theory need have nothing to do with real people as they pass through the stages of life from conception to death. They need not concern the contingent consequences that human actions cause when they occur in regions with different population densities and in environments with different support capacities. Those who accept the naturalistic fallacy make moral knowledge incapable of factual refutation.

Clearly, moral theories have evolved together with the consequences they cause when they direct human affairs. Clearly, ethical theories must pass empirical tests. They are useful when the behavior that they demand causes benefits to outweigh harm. They are mistaken and must be revised or discarded when they demand behavior that destabilizes society or causes a tragic collapse of the environmental commons that sustain moral life.

The error of the naturalistic fallacy is to make-believe that ethical knowledge is to be found in a nonfactual domain where it can have a priori certainty. The belief in the fallacy creates a conceptual gulf between moral behavior on the one hand and the behavior that accords with the laws and physical limits of nature on the other. So conceived, moral theories cannot be limited or refuted by the harm they cause when they direct human affairs. They cannot be refuted by an excessive population, by the destructive exploitation of the environment, or by the damage caused by good intentions. Indeed, to believe that there is a naturalistic fallacy is to disconnect moral knowledge from the changing needs of life and from the changing ability of environments to support it. When a moral theory cannot be refuted by factual evidence, it need have no relevance to life on a finite Earth.

Ethical Theories as Speculation

When a conceptual gulf is assumed to separate moral from factual knowledge, countless theories can be constructed in thought. Moral theories are similar to all other products of human imagination; they can be flights of fancy, mere dreams in the night. As long as they are sequestered in a nonempirical domain of thought, they only have to meet the criterion of validity and coherence with the set of definitions and premises assumed. New empirical data cannot force them to be modified. The harm or damage they cause when they direct human affairs cannot refute them.

Rawls's *A Theory of Justice* is an instance of such speculation. Even the title bears witness to the fact that his concept of justice is merely a theory. He states, "A conception of justice cannot be deduced from self-evident premises or conditions on principles; instead, its justification is a matter of the mutual support of many considerations, of everything fitting into one coherent view."[8] In effect, by considering justification of ethics to be merely a matter of making traditional moral judgments be rational and coherent, he maintains the hubris of ethical rationalism. He takes it for granted that when human reason creates a coherent system of moral judgments out of human-centered sensitivities and time-honored moral convictions, that moral theory gains objective status; it has moral authority; it becomes binding to all mankind.

Again, Rawls stays in the rationalist moral tradition when he assumes that the deliberate act of thinking under a veil of ignorance—a contrived and contrary-to-fact ignorance—allows people to think away their prejudices and gain objective moral knowledge. To be sure, the deliberate attempt to overcome prejudices may eliminate those that people are aware of. But it cannot eliminate those that people are *not* aware of. It cannot eliminate unconscious human-centered moral concepts. These include the cultural and human-centered postulate that only human beings have intrinsic worth and moral standing. This assumption allows people to kill and eat any animal they wish; it allows people to torture and kill animals in medical or scientific experiments, while they judge the similar treatment of any human being to be a moral outrage. The human-centered principles of Western ethics make the moral community an exclusively human community; by definition, it excludes the biological community that life on Earth has created and without which moral life would cease.

Another influential moral philosopher also uses the rationalist model of the NFE to maintain ethics within the domain of a priori thought. In *Freedom and Reason*, Richard Hare attempts to justify moral principles by using "all the powers of thought, imagination, and feeling that a man possesses."[9] By the mistaken belief that reason and mankind's powers of thought, imagination, and feeling are the originating sources of moral knowledge and the sole determinants of moral truth, he affirms a commitment to the rationalist tradition that separates all moral from factual claims.

Again, something is wrong! Regardless of how moral conclusions may be justified in thought, the human mind cannot generate knowledge of the consequences caused by human activity in the physical world. Under conditions of abundant land and natural resources, behavior that accords with Rawls's theory of justice can hold:

that social and economic inequalities, for example, inequalities of wealth and authority, are just only if they result in compensating benefits for everyone, and in particular for the least advantaged members of society. These (moral) principles rule out justifying institutions on the grounds that the hardships of some are offset by a greater good in the aggregate. It may be expedient but it is not just that some should have less in order that others may prosper.[10]

But under conditions of intractable scarcity, the behavior required by Rawl's *Theory of Justice* may disrupt society and cause environments to break down to pioneer states incapable of supporting the moral behavior that his theory requires. It is the arrogance of rationalism to believe that a moral theory that was created by the human mind can determine what happens in the world.

Mere theories, including moral theories, do not determine what happens in nature. Whether they are justified by the considered rational judgments that people make under a veil of ignorance, or whether they are justified by all the powers of thought, imagination, and feeling that man possesses, they are still empty speculation. And they remain so, until they are correlated with actual people and empirical contexts and then used to direct human behavior. When ethical theories direct human affairs, they change what happens in nature. They make empirical predictions. They can benefit mankind under conditions of abundance; they can cause hardship or disaster under conditions of scarcity or environmental collapse. Under conditions of scarcity, societies either modify their ethical theories or else they become extinct.

Rationalism in ethics makes the error of placing moral knowledge in the nonempirical domain, where moral principles can be universally and necessarily true. So conceived, theories of ethics and justice are not subject to any objective factual test: they cannot be refuted by the societal or environmental tragedy they can cause when they direct human affairs. As long as they cannot be refuted by the disastrous consequences caused by overpopulation, or by the environmental breakdown caused by an expanding population and its exploitation of natural resources, all moral theories are mere speculation.

The Distinction between Types of Empirical Knowledge

There are three types of empirical knowledge. The first is knowledge of what is essentially private, particular, and ephemeral. It is knowledge by acquaintance, given directly by introspection, by the sensory experience of individuals. Examples are knowledge of one's headache, one's fear of heights, or the smell of a gardenia in bloom.

The second type is the general empirical knowledge of the characteristics of things and events in the world. Examples are that some roses are red, that water is denser than ice, and that polygamy is legal in Saudi Arabia. To be sure, the second type is less certain than the first, but still it is factual knowledge that can be free, by and large, of personal and cultural bias.

The third is a much more important type of knowledge: it is the knowledge of science—the knowledge of confirmed theory. Examples are that hydrogen combines with oxygen to form water; that natural selection allows the evolution of complex organisms from simpler forms; that germs cause disease; and that specific nutrient, moisture, and light conditions are necessary to a healthy corn plant.

Closer attention needs to be given to the third type of empirical knowledge—scientific and theoretical knowledge. This type of knowledge requires an inductive leap. Generalizations and hypotheses apply to many more instances than the limited data that confirmed them. Knowledge given by generalizations and hypotheses is always tentative—subject to revision or rejection by new factual evidence. Because the confirming data are available to all observers who wish to duplicate it, theoretical knowledge can avoid personal and cultural bias. Its goal is to gain objective empirical knowledge.

Theoretical knowledge can be obtained about the conditions necessary for the maximal development and welfare of maple trees. Although actual maple trees grow in environments that limit their growth and vigor, still it is possible to gain theoretic scientific knowledge of the factual conditions necessary for their health and full development.

Similarly, most people live in societies that stunt their health and development. Still the knowledge of the physical, social, and environmental conditions necessary for human welfare is empirical knowledge. It is available to intelligent observers, even those who might visit the Earth from the planet of a distant star. There is no reason to consider such knowledge to be of a new and entirely different kind, namely, knowledge of ethics.

As a biological species, factual knowledge of human needs and interests include having such necessities as healthy bodies; food with adequate calories, protein, vitamins and minerals; clean water and air; and adequate housing with an indoor climate like that of Africa's high savannas. What is required for the welfare of human beings as intelligent and social animals can also include knowledge of the laws and principles needed to enhance personal, societal, and environmental security; as well as knowledge of the kinds of community that permit leisure, interesting work, and the development of human talents. Thus, although the knowledge of these requirements is varied and complex, it is still theoretical knowledge about one of the Earth's animal species. Empirical evidence can confirm such knowledge for human beings, just as empirical evidence confirms it for maple trees and corn plants.

In summary, the NFE make the logical error of an unjustified, inductive leap. From the premise that moral knowledge differs both from private sensory experience *and* from the knowledge of different moral practices, the NFE make the fallacious inference that moral knowledge differs in kind from theoretical knowledge about the factual needs and interests of human beings as a biological species. By maintaining the mistaken dualism entailed by belief in the naturalistic fallacy, the NFE create a conceptual gulf between moral behavior and the empirical knowledge of the physical conditions necessary for human well-being. This gulf makes it conceptually impossible for moral theories to be refuted by facts— refuted by the disastrous consequences that result when people live by moral principles that are merely hypotheses, and by human-centered values that are merely defined.

In short, the naturalistic fallacy is grounded in the mistaken separation of moral from empirical knowledge. The conceptual gulf that the NFE assume makes it impossible in principle that moral theories be assessed by the contingent factual consequences that result when they guide human behavior. The NFE cannot recognize that moral theories are refuted when they call for behavior that causes ethical theories to die out and environments to break down. To repeat the empirical theme of an ethics for a finite world, nature—not a validly reasoned argument from human-centered moral premises and a human-centered definition of value—is the final determinant of the moral behavior that physical laws and biological limits will permit.

The Method of Conjecture and Refutation

The early modern empiricists grounded empirical knowledge in a conceptual error. They believed that knowledge of the physical world had to be constructed out of the raw data from sensation. Their attempt failed because they disregarded the essential difference between knowledge justified by the immediate data of private sense experience and theoretical knowledge justified by empirical evidence that any interested observer could repeat. Theoretical knowledge that is public and permanent cannot be pieced together out of what is ephemeral and private. It cannot be constructed out of sense data.

Modern science has bridged the gulf between sense data that are private and subjective and the knowledge of confirmed scientific theory that is public and objective. It has invented and developed the hypothetico-deductive method of science. This method allows the definitions, principles, and laws that make up a theory to originate from anywhere, even from intuition or a wild hunch. But before any theory or proposal can have any status in knowledge, the elements of theory must be given an empirical interpretation that allows scientists everywhere to perform the tests that confirm or refute the theory.

The method of conjecture and refutation has proved to be pragmatically useful in gaining knowledge of nature. Over time it allows defective systems of thought to be discarded. It eliminates the divisive effects of different languages, cultures, politics, and the revelations of the one true God. It makes possible the steady accumulation of knowledge in all the fields in which it is applied—in the physical and biological sciences, in engineering and technology, and in medicine. The development of this method of conjecture and refutation is the great contribution of European civilization to mankind. It is high time for it to become the method for gaining knowledge of ethics as well.

Seeing-As and Seeing-Truly

Abstract systems of thought must be interpreted if they are to have any practical significance. For example, Euclidean straight lines and plane figures have their origin in the set of definitions, axioms, and postulates that define plane geometry. All theorems are proved by showing that they follow logically from the primitive assumptions together with the initial conditions that define the problem at hand. The lines, figures, and theorems of plane geometry, however, are fundamentally different from those that occur on the surface of the Earth. Earthly lines and figures have no essential role in justifying geometric theorems. Whatever relevance there is between the two domains cannot be decided by dint of the extraordinary mental effort of great thinkers sequestered in their studies. Rather, the relevance of the theorems of plane geometry to practical problems requires that the lines and figures of abstract geometry be interpreted as lines and figures on the surface of the Earth. When so interpreted, the practical relevance of plane geometry can be tested. Thus, factual evidence proves the relevance of plane geometry to building a house, while it proves the error of its application to large areas of land on the curved surface of the Earth. Although an abstract theory may be useful in one application, it may be false, even disastrous, in another. Lines and figures on the surface of the Earth are not the same as lines and figures in geometric theory.

Another example can be found in a patient's unexpected recovery from a severe illness. The recovery can be interpreted as the benevolent intervention of God. But since unexpected recoveries can have multiple causes, the hypothetical interpretation that God was the cause offers no proof that God exists.

Four-humors medical theory is still another case that is apropos. The theory interprets a high fever to be an instance of excessive sanguinity. It calls for bloodletting to reduce the fever. But this interpretation can prove to be disastrous for the patient. It may, indeed, reduce the patient's fever. But the reduction may be to room temperature—and, unfortunately, it may be permanent.

Closer attention reveals that a similar problem of interpretation exists for ethical theories. When the agents of moral theory are theoretic entities that are defined as being autonomous, interchangeable, and morally equal, it takes little rational ability to deduce that the principles of equal justice, human rights, and philanthropic duties are universal and unconditional. And if the agents of abstract moral theory are interpreted to be actual people, it is easy to deduce that all cases of inequality, discrimination, and unequal treatment are immoral. But the fact that the agents of moral theory can be interpreted to be real people must be tested by factual evidence to determine whether that interpretation causes the expected benefits or whether it causes hardship and societal or environmental tragedy. If to live by an ethical theory causes harm to overwhelm the benefit, that theory is refuted. It must be revised or replaced.

Moral philosophers are similar to engineers and architects in that all can propose designs that they think will serve human needs and interests. Their proposals, however, can fail to take account of the properties of the materials, or fail to conform to the laws and limits of the physical world; it is always possible that their designs can be useless, or even dangerous and absurd.

In ethics, the fact that an uninterpreted moral theory logically entails that human beings (whether they be infants, adults, the aged, or the moribund) all must be treated equally does not prevent their equal treatment from causing a complex of conflicting consequences. Under conditions of excessive and irresponsible reproduction, of pollution on a global scale, or of the destructive exploitation of the environment, to treat all individuals that are genetically human as if they were equal and had equal rights may disrupt society or cause environments to break down. The fact that types of moral behavior have been validly deduced from moral theory has nothing to do with the factual consequences caused by the behavior that a moral theory entails. Thus, when the stipulated agents and circumstances of an ethical theory have been interpreted to refer to real people and real events in nature, empirical tests are necessary to discover whether or not the behavior that the moral theory validly entails will actually cause benefit or will bring harm, even disaster, to society or the environment. Factual evidence is required to determine whether or not a moral theory is suited to direct human activities in a finite world.

In summary, the moral agents and the fundamental laws and principles of an ethical theory must be interpreted before they can have any factual relevance. When the abstract, logical entities of moral theory are taken to refer to real people, their behavior, and actual events in nature, a moral theory may prove to be useful in one context but harmful or dangerous in another. To interpret a moral theory is not to confirm it. Seeing-as is not the same as seeing-truly.

A Thought Experiment about Moral Theories

The fallibility of any ethical theory that is warranted solely by a priori reasoning can be demonstrated by a thought experiment. Imagine an egalitarian ethics of universal human rights and philanthropic obligations that is justified solely by valid reasoning from an anthropocentric definition of value and from moral premises that are merely postulated. Imagine, also, that over a long time span, people discover that to live by this ethics causes them so to exploit and so to damage their environment that human needs, desires, and interests can no longer be met. Under such supposed conditions, can valid arguments ever persuade people of their moral obligation to live by such an ethics? Can abject loyalty to the principles of this ethics be anything other than fanaticism? Won't those who practice such an ethics do one of two things: abandon this ethics and live by a different one, or simply die out and take their hallowed ethics with them? Isn't the evolution of life on Earth grounded in the fact that nature does not allow the deficient and defective to survive? Aren't human moral proposals part of the same evolutionary process? Doesn't nature simply veto faulty human moral practices by allowing them to die out?

The Empirical Basis of the Knowledge of Ethics

The NFE are as unaware as the early modern empiricists of the role of perceived data in justifying theoretic knowledge. Quite correctly, they recognize the gap that separates the perception of personal needs, interests, and preferences from justifiable moral behavior. They also correctly recognize the gap that separates the moral conventions of any society from correct moral behavior. But as long as they use nonempirical criteria to justify moral laws and principles, they fail to understand that the conclusions that are self-evident within the domain of stipulated definitions and assumed premises may have no status in empirical knowledge. The NFE fail to understand that a human-centered definition of value and moral principles postulated by a moral theory may entail moral conclusions that are valid but false. That is, when the individuals and events of moral theory are interpreted to be actual moral agents and actual events in nature, ethical theories can be tested. If factual data support them, or even allow them to be practiced, then they can be accepted, at least tentatively, as a part of moral knowledge. But if factual data proves them to be unsustainable, then they must be revised and tested again or discarded.

Both the early modern empiricists and the NFE fail to understand that the empirical method of proposal and the rejection of failure bridge the gap between the domains of a priori and empirical knowledge. Ethical theories are similar to theories and procedures in medicine. They are acceptable when they cause much benefit and little harm. They are refuted and must be revised or discarded when they cause harm or tragedy to overwhelm any benefit. Just as valid conclusions from medical theory do not necessarily cure patients, so, too, the valid conclusions from moral theories may not increase human welfare; they may even cause a degraded environment to break down. Indeed, ethical and medical theories are similar in that they must be tested by their ability to accomplish the purposes of each discipline. They must be revised and retested or discarded when they allow harm or disaster to overwhelm benefit.

Ethics has empirical tasks to perform. It must build on the environmental principle—the obligation to protect the symbiotically diverse environment in which human beings evolved and which sustains moral life. Then, secondarily, when a durable and resilient environment is secure, moral attention can be directed toward the human goal of making life in society ever more worth living.

The only method for gaining empirical knowledge—knowledge of the factual consequences caused by human activity, including human moral activity—is the experimental method of the natural sciences. When applied to ethics, this method requires that ethical theories be continually assessed by their ability to accomplish the tasks of ethics. Any ethical theory that disregards the environmental principle eliminates itself as a viable ethics. Any ethical theory that violates the secondary principle frustrates the essential purpose of moral life. If any ethics fails in these essential tasks, it is mistaken. It must be revised or discarded.

By adopting the empirical method for gaining theoretical knowledge, people can learn to live within the laws and limits of nature. They can learn how best to limit the human population and restrict the human use of land and natural resources so as to maintain the endurance and resilience of the Earth's biosystem. They can learn how best to structure society so as to make human life ever more worth living. The experimental method will allow a steady increase in the scope and depth of moral knowledge.

Environmental Ethics and the Naturalistic Fallacy

Environmentalists fervently desire to preserve endangered species, coral reefs, mangrove estuaries, old-growth forests, nature reserves, free-flowing rivers, farmlands, and so forth. They will fail, however, as long as they accept the mistaken human-centered conception of ethics that the naturalistic fallacy entails. The argument that supports this conclusion can hardly be faulted.

The naturalistic fallacy builds on the conceptual error of placing moral knowledge in a nonempirical domain where truth can be certain. In this domain, an anthropocentric definition of value and moral laws and principles that are merely assumed, indeed do entail valid moral claims. In the domain of assumed principles and human-centered definition, the principles of equal justice, universal human rights, and the sanctity of human life can be proved to be universal and necessary. In the theoretical domain, valid conclusions will hold, regardless of population densities and regardless of environmental circumstances. They will also entail the duty to relieve all human suffering, to provide sanitary facilities and clean water for everyone, to construct low-cost housing, and to support the global economic development that finds jobs for all human beings at adequate wages. Thus, as long as environmentalists remain ensconced in an ethics that isolates knowledge of what ought to be from possible refutation by factual evidence, the laws and principles of moral behavior are not subject to any factual constraints. They cannot be corrected even when the behavior that present moral theory commands will lead to moral and environmental tragedy. As a consequence, environmentalists will allow vital human needs to trump every environmental concern. Because environmentalists will make one concession after another, dire human needs will convert farms, virgin forests, and available natural resources into factories, mines, housing, parking lots, and intensive monoculture. All moral efforts will be counterproductive. Slowly but inevitably, the moral obligation to satisfy vital human needs will thwart their ability to halt the march of events toward the environmental tragedy that they desire to prevent.

Summary

A revolution was necessary to order to get rid of the ancient Earth-centered misconceptions and establish modern astronomy. One was necessary in order to get rid of the misconception that earth, air, fire, and water were fundamental elements and to establish modern atomic chemistry. One was necessary in order to get rid of the misconception of four humors medical theory and establish modern medicine and the germ theory of disease. A Darwinian revolution is now necessary in ethics in order to get rid of the ancient misconception about the categorical and universal nature of ethics and establish the biological basis of moral life.

As repeatedly noted, moral behavior changes what happens in the world. The knowledge of physical events is empirical knowledge. Such knowledge is gained by proposing and testing generalizations and theories, by retaining what works and rejecting what fails. The empirical, or trial-and-error, method of making proposals and then testing them is also the appropriate method for gaining knowledge of the physical consequences caused by the behavior that moral theory commands. If to live by the laws and principles of an ethical theory causes the breakdown either of society or of the world's biosystem, then those who stubbornly deny the environmental principle simply die out and take their a priori moral convictions with them. Those who survive live by a different ethics. As Darwin demonstrated, evolution is possible when nature weeds out failure. Similarly, the knowledge of ethics can be cumulative and open-ended when ethics is understood to obey Darwinian principles and moral failures can be weeded out and discarded. An ever-fuller knowledge is possible as human beings learn better to fulfill the environmental and human goals of ethics.

Shrader-Frechette, as noted above, states that ethical statements differ in kind from nonethical ones. However, to place ethics in a nonempirical domain of knowledge is to make the evidence that justifies ethical statements differ in kind from the evidence that justifies factual claims. In effect, to believe in the naturalistic fallacy is to believe that non-empirical criteria can yield knowledge of moral laws and principles that hold universally, regardless of the physical consequences that arise when people live as their ethical beliefs command. Clearly, that belief is false. Moral beliefs and theories can be self-eliminating. In effect, a factual state of affairs can nullify and thereby refute them. The fact that empirical evidence can eliminate a moral theory puts moral knowledge in the empirical domain. It proves that moral knowledge cannot be a unique, nonempirical type of knowledge; it demonstrates the fallacy of the naturalistic fallacy.

The Failings of Personal Ethics

In the nations of Europe and the Americas, the assumption is rarely questioned that ethics is personal ethics. So conceived, ethics states the laws and principles that define the dos and don'ts of the moral behavior of individuals. When people follow moral law of their own free will, they are worthy of praise and reward. When they will to defy these laws, they are sinners who deserve punishment.

Personal ethics concerns only the freely willed behavior of individuals. It has no moral concern for human behavior over which individuals have no control. It builds on the assumption that personal moral defects—selfishness, callousness, and greed—are the originating causes of evil in the world. Accordingly, if people of their own free wills choose to guide their lives by the high ideals of personal morality, the world can overcome starvation, disease, terrorism, and war. If mankind could only make the sincere commitment to follow the ideals of personal ethics, an age of peace and well-being would be realized for all mankind.

There are several grounds on which this conception of ethics is limited and mistaken. It errs by placing ethics in the domain of a priori knowledge, where the rules for moral behavior are categorical and universal—a domain in which they cannot be refuted by factual data. It errs by disregarding the fact that it is not individual persons but businesses, organizations, and governments that are the major determinants of human activity. And it errs by being unable to address the environmental causes of human conflict and suffering. Under conditions of scarcity, these failings work together to make hardship, and even moral tragedy, inevitable. Under these conditions, to live by the laws of personal ethics causes consequences that contradict the goals of personal ethics.

Personal Ethics and Moral Law

Most people in the Western nations believe that ethics is the set of laws and duties that govern the moral behavior of individuals. A clear example is found in the Ten Commandments. They state what individuals should not do. When people break moral law, they must be punished; they may even deserve eternal damnation. When they obey moral law of their own free will, they are worthy of praise, even of eternal life. Penalties and rewards—the carrot and the stick—are the blunt and dubiously effective tools for enforcing the laws of personal ethics.

Sins—the personal defects of selfishness, callousness, cruelty, and greed—are held to be the originating sources of evil in the world. If people sin of their own free wills, they are evildoers who must be sought out and brought to justice. It is a moral outrage that an innocent person should suffer or that a sinner should go unpunished.

Because the laws of correct moral conduct are ideals that do not describe actual human behavior, they are commonly justified by nonempirical criteria. For the religious, divine revelation guarantees their supposed absolute authority. For the secular, reason and a priori arguments logically entail their universality and their certainty. In either case, the laws of personal moral conduct are held to be universal in scope and morally obligatory for all mankind.

The Error of the Belief That
Moral Laws and Principles Are Universal and Certain

As noted above in the commentary on terms, two different criteria for truth produce two different domains of knowledge: knowledge in the a priori domain and knowledge in the empirical domain. Because reason and the laws of logic justify a priori knowledge, factual evidence cannot limit or refute that knowledge; it is universal and necessary. On the other hand, because future data may limit or refute any generalizations or hypotheses, empirical knowledge is tentative and contingent.

Knowledge of personal ethics is commonly thought to be a special kind of knowledge whose certainty is universal and unconditional. People commonly accept the fact that laws enacted by governments may be unwise and mistaken. In a democracy they can be corrected. But few people in the Western world ever doubt that the laws and duties of personal ethics differ from the laws of democratic governments in that they are certain and never need to be revised. They can apply in all cultures and under all circumstances. They are the ethics for all mankind.

When an abundance of land and natural resources exists, those who live by the ideals of personal ethics can work to assure that food, shelter, and health care are provided for all mankind. All that is needed is the will and the unselfish dedication to the moral duty to secure the well-being of all mankind. Any failure to do so is proof of moral failure.

If, however, a shortage of land, food, clean water, or energy should ever arise, to enforce the laws of personal moral behavior would cause unexpected consequences. The logic is irrefutable: when an adequate supply of land and vital resources no longer exists, scarcity limits the moral options.

As available land and resources in a finite world become scarce, one option is to follow the rules of personal ethics and give a starvation ration equally and fairly to everyone. Then the slow but inevitable result is the demise of all. The other option is to break the rules of personal ethics and to let some people have the necessities of life while others do without and perish. In a finite world, all those who survive select the second option; they disobey the laws of personal ethics.

Knowledge of the consequences caused by behavior that obeys the commandments of personal ethics is empirical knowledge. Because conditions of intractable scarcity make the practice of this ethics physically impossible, personal ethics is a contingent ethics—it depends on the availability of land and resources to support the conduct. It can never be certain; it can never be final.

The argument is now complete that demonstrates the error of placing the rules of personal ethics in the domain of certain knowledge. Although there are circumstances that allow people to live by the rules of personal ethics, there are other circumstances—a scarcity of land and vital resources—that make such moral behavior physically impossible. Hence, knowledge of the rules of correct personal behavior is contingent. It is a mistake to place personal ethics in the a priori domain where knowledge is unconditional and certain.

The Error of Disregarding the Nonpersonal Human Agencies That Determine Human Behavior

Personal ethics disregards the fact that individual people are no longer the major determinants of human affairs. Now, various human agencies control the course of events on Earth: governments, defense departments, banks, philanthropic foundations, religious organizations, international corporations, and global agreements on free trade establish both the structure and the details of modern life. They are major causes of the present exponential expansion, both in the human population and in the production of consumer goods and services. In turn, expanding human material needs require the increased exploitation of land and resources and cause further damage to an already deteriorating world environment. In the long-term, they make human suffering and strife inevitable.

Because agencies and institutions are not persons, there are no individuals for personal ethics to command; none that it can punish or reward. Although personal ethics maintains the moral authority of the biblical commandment "Thou shalt not kill," it offers no moral guidelines for governing the policies and activities of agencies that are nonpersons. For instance, the moral injunction against murder is of no help to the police or to departments of defense when to carry out their functions will probably cause some people to die. The only questions that confront these agencies are questions of who will die and how the number of casualties can be minimized. Again, personal ethics makes it a duty to aid all those in need, but it offers no rationale to an agency such as The World Bank as to whether or not to fund such major projects as massive dams, mining facilities, agribusiness, and industrial development. In short, the behavior of nonpersonal human agencies falls between the cracks in the code of personal ethics.

Consider a possible case: The World Bank makes a loan for the economic development of an agrarian people. The loan is used to consolidate small farms into larger and more efficient holdings that can produce coffee, tea, cocoa, bananas, or sugar for export on the world market. Such loans increase the income of the developing nation, which can then use the funds to pay for imports of oils and grains. Although consolidated farms can produce products more efficiently, they force small farmers off their lands. And by producing products for export, they do not grow food for local consumption. The displaced farmers are forced to move to the slums and shantytowns of megacities and join the people—now (in 2005) nearly 50 percent of the human population—who now live in the world's major urban areas; there they must have money and buy everything they need. This moral scenario increases the power of multinational corporations to produce and sell vital commodities. It allows international corporations to increase their control over the lives and destinies of people in the developing nations. It increases the gross domestic product. It improves the lives of all who can find employment and who can buy what they need. But it degrades the lives of those who cannot find jobs and can't buy anything.

Are such loans morally justified? Does The World Bank cause some people to starve, while it raises the gross domestic product by greatly increasing the number of the wealthy elite? Is it causing a crime against humanity? If so, who should be sought out and brought before an international court of justice? Who should be punished? Personal ethics is silent. The answers to these questions cannot be deduced from the categorical laws of personal ethics.

Another example is that personal ethics offers no guidelines for dealing with individuals who carry out governmental policies. What moral assessment does personal ethics offer concerning the airmen who dropped atomic bombs on the innocent citizens of Hiroshima and Nagasaki? Is to knowingly burn hundreds of thousands of civilians alive a crime against humanity that has gone unpunished? If so, who is it that is guilty? Is it the airmen who were ordered to drop the atomic bombs? Is it former president Truman, who was the commander in chief that gave the order? Or is it the members of the U.S. congress who voted to fund the war? Again, what is the judgment of personal ethics concerning Adolf Eichmann, who carried out the German government's orders to exterminate Jews? Should individuals be tried personally for the crimes of their governments? Or are they merely functionaries who follow orders? Is it relevant that people who refuse to obey their government's orders would probably be put to death, or at least be replaced by others who do as they are told? Once again, what is the verdict of personal ethics about the violent deaths and destruction done by governments that use military force to crush restive ethnic minorities within their national boarders? What moral rules justify the activities of governments, military forces, religious and philanthropic nongovermental organizations, The World Bank, or the capitalist, free-market system? What regulations are justified and how should they be enforced? Again, the laws of personal ethics either provide no answer to such questions, or, if they do, the answers are either irrelevant or bootless.

To sum up, personal ethics errs on two counts. First, it errs because its narrow focus on personal behavior prevents it from directing the agencies that determine the nature of modern life. Second, it errs because it mistakenly assumes that wrongs will be righted and justice will be served only when guilty individuals are hunted down and punished. Thus, it directs moral attention to a futile search for what often does not exist, namely, guilty individuals who were uniquely responsible for the harm and human suffering that is the goal of moral behavior to prevent. Because it cannot assess or effectively control the activities of the nonpersonal agencies, personal ethics calls for behavior either that is futile or that only exacerbates the evils that it is supposed to redress.

The Inability of Personal Ethics
to Address the Physical Causes of Human Ills

Personal ethics errs in that its categorical moral laws incorporate incentives that only increase human need. Frequently cited examples, again, are apropos.

The obligation of personal ethics to give philanthropic aid to all in need entails counterproductive incentives. The only thing that poor nations have to do in order to receive more aid is to generate more need. Thus, nations with dense populations, high birthrates, and ravaged environments can expect mankind to supply them with the foods and funds they need to relieve their plight. The pragmatic effect of such aid is to subsidize the status quo. It supports the continued growth of the needy population. It stimulates the further destructive exploitation of their degraded environments. Inevitably, the expanding human population and the increased exploitation of the damaged environment cause more people to suffer. Unconditional aid only exacerbates the woes it was intended to redress. The categorical commandments of personal ethics cannot be modified to take account of the fact that the behavior required by personal ethics affects what happens in the world: it can cause hardship and disaster rather than the expected benefit.

When land and natural resources are abundant and the population is small, people can have a great many freedoms—because their activities may well benefit others, or at least bother nobody. For example, those who want large houses with landscaped yards use much fuel and many natural resources to support their way of life. Their expenditures benefit others by increasing employment and profits. Again, parents who have large families increase the diversity both of the workforce and the variety of goods and services that are available to others.

However, when environmental conditions change—that is, when crowding makes land unavailable and causes fuel, water, and the physical necessities to be in short supply—the behavior that the laws of personal ethics command causes adverse and harmful consequences. Then one person's excess use of fuel and natural resources forces others either to use less than their fair share, or even to do without. The excessive consumption of the wealthy takes land, energy, and resources away from the poor. Similarly, extra births in a population that already is at or exceeds its environment's support capacity causes similar harmful consequences. The only difference is that when extra people deprive others of needed food or water, some will not just suffer hardship; they will perish.

Finally, the nonempirical origin of personal ethics makes it disregard the fact that crowding or the lack of food, water, fuel, and facilities for waste disposal can restrict, or even nullify, the laws of personal ethics. When a finite world has to confront physical scarcities, personal ethics has no moral laws to limit births or consumption. Even for parents who are married, it has no laws that make it immoral to have more children than they, the society, and the environment can support. Even when wealthy citizens can afford it, personal ethics has no laws that make it immoral to consume more than one's fair share of material goods and services. The rigid authoritarian laws of personal ethics cannot be revised or discarded, even when to obey them puts society at risk or the environment in jeopardy.

The defect of personal ethics lies in its assumption that the laws of correct personal behavior are universal and categorical. The cause of this inflexibility is to be found in the conceptual error that deliberate human moral error—sin—

is the cause of evil in the world. This error prevents personal ethics from including any laws that make excessive reproduction or excessive consumption immoral. Thus, in a crowded world facing a scarcity of land and natural resources, to live by the rules of personal ethics only increases population growth and promotes environmental decline—the physical causes of human suffering and conflict. This error prevents personal ethics from being able to address the major afflictions that beset the modern world.

Summary

Three sources of error have been found in personal ethics.

First, because personal ethics states the rules of moral behavior that are supposed to be binding on all human beings, these rules must apply in degraded environments and under conditions of physical scarcity. But they can't apply universally! In degraded environments, it is physically impossible to live by the categorical rules of personal ethics, for to do so may cause the demise of all. Nature can demonstrate the failure of ethics as a moral code for personal behavior.

Second, personal ethics errs in that its moral injunctions are irrelevant or futile in directing nonpersonal agencies that now determine the major aspects of modern life. These agencies now support the runaway growth of the world population; they support also the runaway growth of the multinational capitalist system. Such growth, in turn, requires the rapid exploitation of millions of years of the Earth's accumulated natural wealth. It causes a profusion of consumer goods that soon end up as trash and pollution. The narrow focus of personal ethics makes it incapable of controlling the nonpersonal forces that now subvert the goals of moral life.

Third, because personal ethics requires abject obedience to moral laws and philanthropic duties, it ignores the harm, even the moral disaster, that such obedience causes in a finite world in which a scarcity of land and resources is causing the environmental commons to break down. This defect makes it incapable of reducing the human population or of limiting the environmental destruction caused by a growth-oriented economic system. These failings make it impossible for people who live by the laws of personal ethics ever to achieve the ideals of moral life in a finite world that is experiencing the effects of overpopulation and environmental deterioration.

Chapter Three

The Fundamental Principles of an Ethics for a Finite World

Once it is understood that nature can veto any moral code that human beings propose to live by, the character of ethics changes. It breaks with the time-honored tradition that ethics is human centered, that only human beings have moral status and are worthy of moral consideration. It gives moral theory an environmental foundation. By preventing the needs and interests of human beings from overwhelming those of all other things in the biological community, ethics is biocentric.

- Although all living things are members of the moral community, they do not have equal status. Their status varies with their role in fulfilling the environmental and human goals of ethics.

- Because all natural resources in a finite world are limited, the human use of these resources must be limited to what a healthy and enduring biosystem can sustain. Because they require food, biological resources, land, and energy to live, all human beings have materially dependent value. In environments with abundant land and resources, extra people increase human well-being. In deteriorating environments with an excess population, extra people decrease human well-being. In devastated and overpopulated environments, people lose value. Their value may become negative.

• All moral rules that require the use of matter or energy must be adjusted to suit the quantity of resources available to support the behavior that moral rules require. They can allow many human rights and freedoms when open lands and untapped resources are abundant. They severely restrict human rights and freedoms when resources are scarce.

• The poverty or wealth of the environment—not mere membership in the human race—determines the rights, duties, and freedoms that it is physically possible for people to have.

Chapter three has a constructive task: it is to make explicit specific principles that are entailed by the environmental and human goals of ethics. In a finite world, moral behavior must recognize both physical and biological constraints. Because modern man is rapidly exploiting the natural wealth that it took the Earth millions of years to create, the evidence is mounting that a rapid environmental decline is now occurring on a global scale. For the first time in geological history, one of the Earth's creatures—mankind—is upsetting the world biosystem and causing it to collapse to a simpler, pioneer state, which is unlikely to be able to support much longer either the present human population or the present growth-oriented economic system.

Hence, it is becoming more and more urgent that ethical

theory be grounded in the environmental principle. It will be an ethics that entails a different concept of good and evil; it will use different criteria to distinguish moral from immoral behavior. Its primary task is to maintain a healthy, durable, and resilient world environment. It will require that the human population be reduced to numbers that the renewable resources of the Earth can support. It will also require the human use of these resources to remain safely below levels that allow for the vagaries of floods, droughts, and natural calamities. Once the primary goal is secure, the secondary, human goal may be addressed. This goal is to structure human societies and to direct individual behavior so as to improve the quality of human life and make it ever more worth living.

The following principles are essential to the environmental and human goals of an ethics for a finite world.

Two Kinds of Value
Some values are nonmaterial; they use little more matter or energy than that required for normal living. Other things and activities that are valued, however, are materially dependent. Because they often use significant extra amounts of matter and energy, they can exist only if the material resources are available to support them.

Instances of the first kind of value include knowledge, information, education, cultural and artistic achievements, and goodwill toward and respect for other people. They also include many of the service values of entertainment, telecommunication, and information storage and retrieval, which are now spurring economic growth.

Instances of the second kind are found in the many

materially dependent things and activities that are highly valued. They include food, housing, travel, professional sports, experimental research, medical care, educational facilities, and having and raising children.

To gain values of the first kind is a plus-sum game; they can be shared and expanded indefinitely. But values of the second type are zero-sum values; any of these values that are gained by one person are denied to all others. For example, the food you eat cannot feed the destitute. The gasoline that runs your car cannot run your neighbor's. If a player is at bat in the game of baseball, no other players can bat until the batter is out, gets to base, or scores. The money that funds your research does not support anyone else's.

Of the usual grounds for justifying traditional values—appeals to reasoned arguments, to equality and justice, to the ideals of the great religions, to the obligation to relieve human suffering—none can create new material resources. Moral principles cannot increase any of the materially dependent values when the necessary physical resources do not exist.

Furthermore, experience determines which of various materially dependent values are incompatible with others. To clear more land for farms conflicts with conserving forests. Needed housing developments destroy agricultural fields. When materially dependent values conflict, ethical theory must decide which ones to select and which ones to deny. It is not reason or moral principles but rather factual evidence about the availability of matter, space, and energy that determines the type and the quantity of materially dependent values that are compatible with each other in a finite world.

Inevitably, when ethics concerns materially dependent

values, it is a hard-nosed discipline whose often-heartrending task is to justify giving material resources to some worthy individuals or species and denying them to others. The best way to minimize or avoid the wrenching moral problems caused by scarcity is to enforce physical constraints that limit these values. Moral theory must assure that a desperate shortage of land or material resources never makes it necessary to reduce or deny materially dependent values, and especially the value of human beings. These decisions must be grounded in factual knowledge about the quantity of material resources that the Earth can provide for sustained human use. They must constantly be tested to make sure that they fulfill the environmental and human goals of moral life.

Trade-Offs and Materially Dependent Values

It is important to emphasize that materially dependent values are conditional values, not intrinsic ones. A finite world is a world of limits. It prevents any materially dependent values from expanding exponentially. Thus, the human population cannot continually increase; also, more schools, hospitals, medical facilities, universities, research centers, libraries, cultural centers, parks and sport arenas, municipal water systems, and the other materially dependent values cannot continue to be built. The land and resources given to one cannot be given to anything else of materially dependent value.

When the demand for land and resources stresses any environment, conditions of scarcity arise. Scarcity then changes the nature of ethics. To give resources to one means that those resources must be denied to all others. Impending scarcity changes the nature of ethics. It makes the fundamental problem of ethics become how to justify the trade-offs of materially dependent values. An ethics for a finite world must make sure that conditions of scarcity do not arise that will necessitate trade-offs that thwart the goals of moral life.

Points of Moral Reversal

Hardin recognized that ethics must take account of numbers and quantities. In *The Ostrich Factor*, he states that by the journalistic ploy of coining the term global village,

> the popular understanding of ethics was once again freed from the embarrassing burden of scale effects. Ethical principles developed for a community of ten dozen citizens were lightly assumed to be no different from the principles needed for a world of 5 thousand million people. Unmentioned was the fact that scale effects necessarily shape the default positions of theories that deal with the interactions of large numbers of people.[1]

And later he summarizes this claim: "In ethics, as in all other forms of (scientific) knowledge, numbers matter."[2]

To be sure, under conditions of abundant land and natural resources, everyone benefits when people act according to the commonly accepted moral ideals. But in the essay "Carrying Capacity as an Ethical Concept," Hardin correctly notes:

> The morality of an act is a function of the state of the system at the time the act is performed—this is the foundation stone of situationist, ecological ethics. ... The interests of posterity can be brought into the reckoning of ethics if we abandon the idea

of the sanctity of (present) life as an absolute ethical ideal, replacing it with the idea of the sanctity
of carrying capacity.[3]

As the population increases, or as the environment
becomes more stressed, conditions of scarcity force fundamental changes in moral behavior. If everyone acts according to the same moral rule, the behavior that once produced
only benefit begins to cause harm and damage instead. The
point at which the changeover occurs can be called the point
of moral reversal. It is the point at which to follow a given
rule or law turns from causing much benefit and little harm
to causing harm to overwhelm all benefit. To continue to
follow the same rule of moral behavior may eventually cause
irreversible disaster. Behavior that conforms to a rule or law
changes from being moral to being immoral.[4]

Many examples support this empirical claim. As more
and more people graze their animals on finite commons, as
more and more people use land and biological resources to
satisfy their basic human needs, fewer resources remain for
each person and for all the other living things. Then, as the
resources dwindle, the biological commons collapse to a
simple, pioneer state that can no longer supply human needs.

The freedom to use the oceans as a common resource
gives everyone the right to fish. Initially, everyone benefits
from the activities of fishermen. But as more and more people
fish in the ocean commons, the catches decline and the costs
of fishing begin to equal and then to exceed the profits.
Finally, the harm of fishing predominates when overfishing
causes the fish stocks to crash and everybody to lose. Then
fishing changes from causing benefit to causing harm. It
changes from being moral to being immoral.

Another example comes from the modern diet. Human beings are genetically designed to like sweets and fats. The affluence of the people in industrial societies has allowed them to eat vast quantities of these cheap and readily available foods. The result is that many people suffer from obesity and diminished health. Again, there is a point of value reversal for a diet of sweets and fats. To eat sweets and fats changes from producing benefit to causing harm, from being beneficial to being harmful.

Further cases demonstrate that points of moral reversal are inevitable: the burning of coal in the houses of London; the use of groundwater for irrigation; the use of pesticides in agribusiness; the cutting of timber in virgin forests; the suburban housing developments; the driving of private cars in major cities; the burning of fossil fuels, which pump carbon dioxide into the atmosphere; and giving birth to children in crowded and environmentally degraded lands. In sum, as activities that use land, material resources, or energy reach a point of moral reversal, they turn from producing benefit to causing harm; they turn from being moral to being immoral.

Because human life is a materially dependent value, the human population increase deserves further attention. Human beings, like all other animals on Earth, live only by destroying the biological resources that other living things—ultimately, the plants—create. Because the Earth is finite, and because photosynthesis allows plants to produce only a finite quantity of biomass, biological demands of human beings can increase to the point that the environment can no longer supply the biological resources that people require. At that point, the lifeboat analogy that Hardin made famous is apropos.[5] If the load of passengers aboard a lifeboat brings sea level near the gunnels, then to add extra people for any reason endangers the lives of all. The finite Earth is similar to an overcrowded lifeboat: extra people can so exploit the Earth's land and resources that they put the value of everyone in jeopardy.

The concept that human life is a materially dependent value contradicts the commonly accepted moral conviction that every human life is precious, every life equal in intrinsic value. Human lives, however, can have value only as long as land, food, energy, and material resources are available to support them. When the material resources do not exist adequately to support a population, human beings lose their preciousness and their human rights. Extra people, whether added by birth or by immigration, change from increasing the goods and services available per capita to decreasing them. A growing population eventually causes people to become poverty-stricken and desperate. Life becomes cheap: parents sell their children into servitude and prostitution; theft, extortion, kidnapping, and murder become the available means of survival. To slightly modify the phrase that Thomas Hobbes made famous, life becomes crowded, poor, nasty, brutish, and short.[6] A growing human population in any finite domain eventually causes human life to lose all value.

Only empirical evidence can determine when conditions of overcrowding and scarcity cause human activities to reach the point of moral reversal. Empirical evidence also determines the severity and extent of the moral constraint on human numbers and activities necessary to avoid reaching that point. Moral constraint that limits the quantity of materially dependent values is, thus, a necessary condition for fulfilling the goals of moral life.

Nature's Veto of Moral Theories

Moral behavior takes place within the Earth's finite biosystem. Moral agents die and new ones are born. Population densities vary and environmental systems evolve. Inevitably, ethical theories must take account of the fact that both moral agents and biological conditions are materially dependent values. Neither remains constant through time and circumstances. Hence, no moral rules that concern living organisms or evolving ecosystems can be eternal, universal, or invariant. They must be altered to accommodate changes in the quantity of material resources that are available to sustain them.

Although modern technology has vastly increased the energy and natural resources that people can exploit, human beings create nothing. They live only by killing other living things, by using the biological resources of the Earth, and by using the energy that the Sun provides. Inevitably, moral behavior is dependent on the availability of the material resources necessary to support that behavior. Thus, if human moral behavior should need more energy and resources than nature can sustain, human beings have only two options. One option is to continue to live by the supposed infallible and universal moral principles until the destructive exploitation of the environment causes it to break down and the population to crash. In the crash, the ethics that caused it becomes extinct. The other option is to modify their ethical theory to include principles that limit the human population and the human exploitation of resources to what the Earth's environment can sustain.

The mere fact that moral behavior was deduced from a moral theory that was justified by validly reasoned arguments from human-centered moral principles and a human-centered definition of value has nothing to do with nature's ability or inability to support the behavior that such a moral theory demands. The moral theories that survive are ones that make moral behavior conform to the laws and limits of nature. Any theory that requires moral behavior to violate the laws or limits of nature eliminates itself; it is futile. Inevitably, factual tests determine whether or not an ethics is suited to guide human affairs in a finite world. Nature's veto of a moral theory is final.

Ethics as Biocentric

If only human beings have intrinsic value and moral status, then ethics is human centered. No nonhuman organisms have intrinsic value. None have moral standing in their own right; none are worthy of moral consideration. Such a human-centered ethics can impose no moral restrictions on the way people treat the environment or other living things. People's use of the nonhuman resources of the Earth falls outside the moral domain. Because Western ethics states no laws or principles that limit human numbers, human needs, or the human exploitation of nature, this ethics allows all materially dependent human values to expand indefinitely. Inevitably, it allows people to use any resource and to sacrifice any nonhuman organism as long as the use or sacrifice fills some human need or interest.

Again, the environmental principle is apropos. An exponentially expanding demand for the material resources of a finite world eventually impoverishes the land and depletes its resources. Ever-increasing exploitation causes the environmental commons to collapse to a simpler, pioneer state incapable of supporting the human activity that caused the breakdown. Thus, whenever empirical evidence confirms that an environmental collapse is immanent, the only ethical systems that can survive are ones that impose moral constraints on all human activity. The fact that an enduring and self-sustaining system of living things is a necessary condition for moral life refutes the moral principle that human beings and their interests are the sole concern of ethics. The ethical systems that survive acknowledge the moral priority of the Earth's biological community over human needs and interests, as well as those of every organism within it.

Thus, all living things have some moral standing in the moral community; all are players in the game of ethics. But not all players are keystone players. Empirical evidence proves that many species are dispensable. Still, the endurance and resilience of the moral community is a prerequisite for moral life. That fact makes the Earth's biological system, which living things have created and now maintain, a life-centered rather than a human life–centered moral community. Ethics is biocentric.[7]

Equal Membership in the Moral Community but Not Equal Status for All Members

Being a member of the moral community does not entail the conclusion that all members have an equal moral status. The biological evidence is undeniable that not all organisms have equal roles in maintaining the biosystem. The evidence is equally clear that not all human beings have equal roles in maintaining society and its economic, governmental, policing, cultural, and research functions. What is unequal by nature cannot be made equal by legislation or moral fiat. Equal membership in the moral community does not entail equal moral status.

By analogy, the market price of all vital goods and services cannot be made identical by moral fiat or governmental decree. Rather, the scarcity of resources and the varying costs of producing goods and services must be reflected in different prices. To trade in goods and services that have different values requires only that they be priced in the same currency.

The situation is similar for allotting the available land and resources among the Earth's different individuals and species. Although the needs and interests of the various organisms differ widely in their needs, their abilities, and their contributions to the biosystem, still, they are all elements of the same biosystem; they must be comparable—priced in the same currency. Their relative status must be set according to the role each species plays in maintaining the health, the durability, and the resilience of the whole. No ad hoc or arbitrary moral definitions can make individuals identical when they, in fact, are not. Human beings cannot presume that their knowledge of the workings of the biosystem is adequate or correct.

All proposals about the degree of moral status to be accorded to the different species and different individuals within an ecosystem are empirical proposals. Some individuals and some species are keystone players; others sit on the sidelines. The moral status of individuals and species varies according to the role each plays in fulfilling the moral tasks of maintaining the durability and resilience of the biosystem. No living thing has a moral status that is unchanging and final.

Moral Constraint as an
Essential Condition for Moral Life

When moral principles are assumed to be defining characteristics for the human species, it is clearly valid to conclude that every member of the human race is morally equal, that every human being has the same moral duties, and that human rights are universal. But valid conclusions from a moral definition and human-centered moral assumptions cannot create suddenly out of nothing the land and biological resources needed to satisfy the vital needs of any human population—regardless of the population's size and regardless of its destructive exploitation of the land within its national boundaries. Inevitably, when a population exceeds the capacity of an ecosystem to support it, both individuals and species compete for vital resources. Severe scarcity makes it physically impossible for all to survive.

It is a fundamental characteristic of all life-forms on Earth that they strive to preserve themselves and to expand the domain of their species. Without this disposition, individuals would not survive and species would not evolve. Human beings are no exception. But the species-furthering success of the human race is exactly the cause of its present predicament. Modern technology has made mankind the Earth's dominant species. E. O. Wilson states, "We already appropriate 40 percent of the planet's organic matter produced by green plants."[8] The finitude both of the Earth and of the energy from the Sun makes it improbable that human beings can continue much longer to increase their exploitation of land, energy, and biological resources. Soon, the human population and its production of goods and services will reach steady state, or the Earth's biosystem will crash and bring modern civilization down with it.

The system that nature has devised over the last billion years is likely to be more durable and stable than any that human beings can devise to replace it. Can anyone justify an ethics whose goal is to maximize the number of people who can live on Earth all at once—now—and thereby cause the Armageddon of a biological collapse? Isn't it a wiser ethics whose goal is to maximize the number of people who can live on Earth over the next billion years?

Within the limits set by the needs of a resilient and enduring biosystem, ethical theory may allow human values and interests to have the highest status in the world's biological community. The highest status in the moral community, however, does not give human needs an unconditional priority over the needs and interests of all other species that make up the Earth's biosystem. In fact, an ethics suited to a finite world must recognize that nature allows humankind only a narrow range of options in the use of land and resources. It behooves humankind to proceed carefully and with near certainty that nature can sustain the human use of the Earth's lands and resources. Any miscalculation can lead to an environmental breakdown that is likely to be forever. Such a breakdown—whether deliberate or unintended—would be empirical proof that the ethics that allowed it to happen was mistaken. Ethics must be founded on the environmental principle. It requires strict constraints on both human reproduction and on the human exploitation of land, energy, and resources. Humanly enforced moral constraint is a fundamental and necessary condition for moral life in a finite world.

Human Actions, not Human Genes, as the
Warrant for Human Rights, Duties, and Opportunities

When nations allow their populations and/or their exploitation of land and resources to stress their environments, they reduce its support capacity as well as its ability to sustain a high quality of life. Conversely, in nations that maintain their population and their use of land and resources at levels that their national boundaries can sustain, their citizens can have a high quality of life; they can have the amenities of life: they can enjoy bodily comforts, leisure, cultural activities, and the freedom to travel.

However, nations that have an excessive population must decrease their use of all material resources. They must restrict bodily comforts, travel, cultural activities, and the facilities that support education and research in science and medical care. In fact, all materially dependent rights and freedoms must be curtailed in order to provide for the vital needs of the dense population. Thus, the rights, freedoms, and opportunities of people in overpopulated nations cannot be the same as those of the citizens of nations that *hold their populations stable and live within the support capacities of their national boundaries.*

The general conclusion is inevitable: the fact that human beings all share human genes and are members of the same logical class does not give the citizens of all nations equal rights, opportunities, and freedoms. Valid deductions from moral theory cannot create the physical resources necessary to provide these materially dependent values for everyone. Rather, it is the wealth or poverty of environments that determines how citizens must live. It is what they do—how many children they have, how they use their land, energy, and resources, and how they protect their environments—

that determines the opportunities, rights, freedoms, and the quality of life that are possible in their finite environments.

Contingent Rules for Moral Behavior

Ethical theory must allow the rules of moral behavior to change according to both the size of the human population and the amount of land, energy, and material resources that nature allows people to exploit sustainedly. As has often been noted, both increases in the human population and decreases in the environment's support capacity change the consequences that follow from enforcing the same code of moral behavior. In the modern world, overpopulation and environmental decline are soon to become the major causes of human conflict and suffering. They can overwhelm the personal defects of greed, selfishness, and cruelty as major causes of disease, turmoil, and tragedy in the modern world. Inevitably, in order to fulfill the goals of moral life, every nation has the moral obligation to control its population and to limit the use of its lands, fuels, and material resources to quantities safely below the maximum support capacity of its environment. These moral tasks now take precedence over the traditional commandments of personal ethics, which in the Western world are commonly assumed to be the fundamental principles of ethics.

Chapter Four
Proposals to Further the Goals of Ethics

Chapter four has a practical task: it is to propose laws and moral principles that can be tested to see if they promote the environmental and societal objectives. There is no presumption that the following are correct or that they are new or original. However, once people understand that factual knowledge is needed of the contingent consequences caused by moral behavior, they will be encouraged to think up other proposals that can be tested. Some proposals may be effective and easily enforced. Others may prove to be cumbersome, unenforceable, or even counterproductive. Only trial-and-error evidence can determine whether or not any proposal furthers the environmental principle, whether or not it helps to design a society that makes human life more worth living. All illustrate the creative and evolving nature of ethics.

It must constantly be kept in mind that an ethics for a finite Earth must reject the rationalist misconception of the nature of ethics. It simply is false that human reason and traditional moral judgments, even when they are coherent and seemingly unbiased, can establish the moral laws and principles that are universal and binding for all mankind. By contrast, moral behavior must be flexible. It must change when it causes hardship and harm instead of the expected benefit.

As a consequence, even the most revered principles of Western ethics are conditional. For instance, the right to marry and have children, the monogamous family, free speech, freedom of religion, private property, democratic government, private free enterprise, universal human rights, human equality and equal justice, the right to national defense, and the liberty of nations to determine their own internal affairs are all conditional. Because, almost invariably, they require a transfer of matter or energy, they may be appropriate under some circumstances and inappropriate or even dangerous under others. They can be retained only when they are conducive to the long-term benefit of society and the environment. They are absurd when they cause harm or disaster to overwhelm benefit. Their appropriateness to guide human affairs is a function both of the density of the population and the health and resilience of the environment.

The world has a rapidly growing human population, a stressed and deteriorating global environment, and a world economic system dedicated to the rapid expansion of the production of material goods and services. Now, however, the almost-universal commitment to the ideal of constant growth threatens to destabilize both the local and the world environments; it also threatens to destabilize society and thwart the goals of moral life. An ethics designed for life on this finite Earth must recognize that causation works in human affairs: you tend to get what you subsidize. If you need to stop population growth, you must stop encouraging and subsidizing it. If you need to preserve the durability and resilience of the world environment, you need to stop promoting the unsustainable and destructive exploitation of its lands, fossil fuels, and mineral and biological resources. Hence, ethics must have laws and incentives to scale back both the human population and the economic system to quantities that an enduring and resilient biosystem can sustain.

In short, moral law and political policies must be grounded in the environmental principle. Then, when the environment is secure, their goal is to encourage people to devise a society that promotes social, aesthetic, intellectual, cultural, and recreational values. The moral challenge will always remain to simplify human material needs, to lessen the human demand on the Earth's lands and biological resources, and to expand society's ability to make human life ever more worth living.

I. The Global Village Is a Self-Negating Ideal

To be sure, global policies must be enforced that preserve the ocean fisheries, the ozone layer, the stability of the atmosphere, biological diversity, and the durability and resilience of the Earth's ecosystems. The United Nations, or some international authority, must get the nations of the world to agree on global environmental laws and on the means to enforce them.

However, the concept of the global village as it is commonly conceived has a different thesis. It holds that all mankind forms a single moral community in which all citizens have common entitlements, freedoms, rights, and duties. So conceived, mere membership in the global community gives all citizens a right to food, medical care, clean water, housing, and employment at a living wage. As Virginia Abernethy notes, "So within one-world, help would be the right of poor nations and a duty of the richer ones."[1] In effect, any failure to satisfy these common human needs breaks the bonds of community.

As long as membership in the global community accords to everyone in the world equal rights without corresponding responsibilities, it has a built-in defect. The defect is that all citizens of the global community have the same rights, freedoms, and opportunities no matter what they do or have done, no matter where they live, and no matter what their religion or family conventions may be. In effect, human genes determine people's moral status rather than their actual behavior.

For example, the citizens of nations whose runaway population has destroyed their environment's ability to support them can still expect to have the same freedoms, education, health care, and access to employment and vital necessities that the other citizens of the global community have. Furthermore, when people are assured that they have equal access to the necessities of life, few incentives remain for them or their nation to change their behavior, to reduce their fertility rates, to reform their religious practices, to revise their economic system, or to work to provide for their own needs. Because all people are equal members of the global community, overpopulated nations can continue to export their citizens to the less-crowded lands.

Just as the citizens of the United States can live in any state they wish, so the citizens of the global community have the right to live in any country they please. Then, as Herman Daly has noted, free immigration

> would lead to massive relocation of people between world regions of vastly differing wealth, creating a tragedy of the open commons. The strain on local communities, both the sending and the receiving, would be enormous. In the face of

unlimited migration, how could any national community maintain a minimum wage, a welfare pro-
gram, subsidized medical care, or a public school
system? Indeed, one wonders, would it not be
much cheaper to encourage emigration of a country's poor, sick, or criminals, rather than run welfare programs, charity hospitals, and prisons?
(Fidel Castro took precisely this course of action in
opening Cuba's jails in 1980 … [Prisoners became]
part of the wave of 'marielito' immigrants to the
United States).[2]

Or, alternatively, in order to maintain the flow of aid in
the form of food, medicine, clean water, and capital for economic expansion, impoverished nations only have to generate more need. As long as such aid is forthcoming, there is
no reason or incentive for people to change their ways—to
reduce their fertility rates or learn to live within the support
capacities of their national environments. By disregarding
the destructive effects of an expanding population or of an
increased exploitation of the world's finite land and
resources, the global village voids all the sanctions by which
nature maintains a durable, stable, and self-regulating biological community.

In summary, the pragmatic effect of the single global
community is to promote the status quo of dependency and
overpopulation and to subsidize environmental abuse.
Without constant constraints on population growth and on
economic expansion, the global village will exploit the
resources of the global commons until it breaks down to a
pioneer state incapable of supporting its human population.
In effect, to enforce the ideals and principles of a single

world community is to cause its eventual demise. The global community is, indeed, a dangerous and self-negating ideal.

2. Nations and Peoples
Make Their Own Moral-Cultural Experiments

Nature designed an experimental method that has made possible the evolution of life on Earth. Sexual reproduction offers many genotypes, while competition between individuals and species favors the well adapted by allowing them better to survive and reproduce. The same method can also assure moral and political progress.

History is the account of the rise and fall of civilizations. As previously noted, Diamond attributes their downfall to their inability to live within the support capacity of their various environments.[3] The trial-and-error method that has permitted the evolution of life on Earth suggests that nations and peoples make their own cultural experiments. In effect, civilizations select the population size, the degree of urbanization, and the stress they place on the land and resources of their environments. Their experiments fail if they embody economic, political, or moral incentives that exhaust the resources of the environments that support them. They also fail if they cannot give their citizens a quality of life that they can accept. The autonomy of nations to make their own moral experiments prevents the fate of all humankind from being decided by a single, fallible global experiment.

The lifeboat analogy of Hardin can be modified to make it relevant to the danger of a single global village ideal.[4] The ideal is similar to a ship with a single lifeboat. If there is a shipwreck and the passengers are in one lifeboat, the boat may founder and all may be lost. But if there is a fleet of lifeboats, at least some boats are likely to weather the storm. Nature's method of creating multiple genotypes has made possible the evolution of life on Earth. A similar method of allowing multiple independent societal experiments allows the better-adapted societal experiments to survive.

The ideal of a single global human community builds on the principle that all citizens of the world community have equal rights and opportunities. Such a community is intrinsically unstable because it incorporates incentives that cause its own demise. The high birthrates of needy nations entitle them continually to export their excess population to less-populated nations. Nations that have trashed the lands within their national boundaries impose a duty on the global community to bring humanitarian aid to their needy citizens in order to give them a standard of living equal to that of the other citizens of the world community. The steady flow of populations out of overpopulated regions and the steady flow of humanitarian aid into devastated environments work together to create a dangerous situation. They force the less-populated areas to become more densely populated; they force the world's material resources to be exported to devastated environments. The end point of these processes is a world with the highest-possible population density and with all its environments equally degraded. Such a global community has the incentives that give rise to Hardin's tragedy of the commons. The expanding needs of the global community so stress the Earth's biosystem that it collapses to a simpler state incapable of supporting the global community that caused the collapse. Such a community incorporates the seeds of its own demise.

By contrast, when there are many experiments with

different population densities, different standards of living, and different rights and freedoms, some experiments will be more successful than others in fulfilling the goals of ethics. But the freedom to make such experiments entails the moral obligation of each nation to accept the consequences of that freedom. Autonomous nations must be allowed to carry out their own cultural experiments without incurring the moral obligation to rescue the nations whose misguided experiments have failed. The autonomy of nations requires them to be self-reliant and self-supporting. To a degree that does not violate the environmental principle, the citizens of all nations have to experience the destructive consequences of their own experiments in order to learn how to correct them and better to fulfill the goals of moral life.

3. Immigration Is Strictly Limited

If nations and peoples are allowed to work out their own moral, economic, and cultural experiments, human rights and moral obligations need to be limited. That is, people of overcrowded nations have no moral right to immigrate to other countries; nations that live by the environmental principle have no moral obligation to give their natural wealth to those that have squandered their resources and trashed their environments. No nation has the obligation to share its material resources or the products of its land equally and justly with the citizens of other nations.

Any nation that does not limit immigration loses its ability to make its own cultural/moral experiment. Its failure to curtail immigration would prevent it from choosing to use its lands and natural resources to support a minimal population at a high standard of living and a maximum quality of life. In effect, uncontrolled immigration allows nations whose experiments have failed to overload the world lifeboat and cause it to founder.

It is important to stress that to prevent the citizens of overcrowded nations from becoming permanent residents of less-populated countries is not racism or imperialism. Rather, it is a logical consequent of the finitude of every nation's boundaries. Inevitably, the land and resources of every nation have a maximum support capacity at any given standard of living. When a nation has maximized the exploitation of the renewable resources within its boundaries, it cannot allow immigrants to come in, reduce the per-capita natural wealth, and diminish the standard of living of all the citizens of the host country. That is, immigrants cannot be allowed to deprive—to rob—the citizens of the receiving country of their open lands and natural resources and force them to reduce the resources they use to support cultural, educational, and research activities. To repeat, this is not cultural or racial prejudice; rather, it is a logical consequence of the fact that people live in a finite world—a world in which citizens become desperate when their rapidly rising numbers exceed the capacity of their environments to sustain them.

All citizens who feel morally outraged by the necessity of restricting immigration should they themselves volunteer to emigrate; their emigration will enable them to yield their favored place in their nation to someone who is desperate and oppressed. If they cannot find any nation to accept them, they might consider euthanasia for themselves because the vacancy they create would give some desperate individual the opportunity for a better life.[5]

Inevitably, the finitude of the world causes overpopulation and environmental degradation to become desperate possibilities. Every nation must take moral and legal responsibility for its own fertility rate, for the size of its own population, and for the preservation of its lands and resources. To do otherwise would only assure that no nation can retain a low population and protect its national parks and wildlife preserves from continual exploitation. No! An ethics suited to a finite world cannot cause all nations to become equally overpopulated and their environments equally degraded. Rather, the environmental principle places a moral obligation on every nation to maintain its fertility rates and its use of land and natural resources safely below levels that its national boundaries can sustain. The environmental principle limits the right to immigrate in a finite world.

4. The Importation of Fuels, Timber, and Minerals from Other Nations Is Restricted

The industrialized nations of the world now are the major consumers of the world's fuel, mineral, and biological resources. They are also the major sources of world pollution. The billions of the world's poor do only a small fraction of the environmental damage caused by merely hundreds of thousands of the citizens of wealthy industrialized nations.

The United States is the greatest offender of the environmental principle. Needy and developing nations trade their raw materials for dollars—U.S. government debt. Having already used up much of its own natural wealth, the United States now sucks in needed raw materials from all over the world: petroleum, natural gas, timber, aluminum, copper, nickel, platinum. The figures commonly cited are that the United States has less than 5 percent of the world's population and yet consumes between 25 and 40 percent of the world's resources.

Many people—perhaps even most—are mesmerized by the power of multinational corporations, global trade, and the free-market system to expand the production of material goods and services. They consider economic expansion to be a natural process that cannot be stopped. They claim that it benefits all mankind, rich and poor nations alike. But this claim is far from the case. The billions of dollars that the industrialized nations pay for the raw materials go only to the governments of developing nations or to multinational corporations. Very little benefit filters down to needy citizens. Furthermore, almost all of the governments of impoverished but resource-rich nations are despotic regimes. They vary from military dictatorships to governments run by a type of mafia. They use the income from the sale of raw materials to buy armaments to keep them in power. They damage native environments and threaten the lives of indigenous peoples.[6]

As Senator Kerry has declared, the United States should be self-sufficient in energy. To make that happen, however, the United States will have to stop the importation of fossil fuels that it uses to run its electric-power plants and its cars, trucks, ships, and airplanes. To be energy self-sufficient is not a simple task. It will require that the United States will have to reduce its use of petroleum by 50 percent. Its profligate consumerist way of life will be have to be restructured and simplified.

The environmental principle and the right of nations to make their own moral/cultural experiments work together to require nations to became largely self-sufficient. Nations cannot be allowed to import fuel and natural resources from all over the world, turn them into material goods and services, export them to earn money, and then use the money earned to buy more fuel and natural resources and start the production and resource-exploitation cycle all over again. The reason that moral constraints must be placed on global free trade can be simply argued: unrestricted global free trade fosters continual expansion; it has no principles that limit population growth or that conserve the Earth's natural resources. In effect, it allows both population and economic production to expand until they deplete all material resources worldwide and the world commons collapse to a simpler, pioneer state that cannot sustain the global community. It is the economic counterpart of forcing all mankind into the same foundering lifeboat.

By contrast, the environmental principle requires that nations reduce their use of energy to quantities that their national boundaries can sustain. Nations should trade only what they produce in excess of their needs. They can then trade their excesses for the materials and products that they cannot readily produce for themselves. To be sure, standards of living would differ widely around the world, but the autonomy of nations would be increased. Desperately poor nations would not be driven to sacrifice their national resources and degrade their environments in order to support the expanding global economy until it collapses.

Furthermore, if the people of the United States exploit only products manufactured from the renewable resources from within its national boundaries, the economic pressure that the United States exerts on the impoverished and non-industrialized peoples of the world would be greatly diminished. Multinational corporations would no longer be a modern version of the colonial powers of Europe in the sixteenth through nineteenth centuries that exploited and enslaved the people of Africa and the Americas. The United

States would have to learn how to devise an acceptable way of life for its citizens that would be free of the need to pollute distant environments and to cause indigenous peoples either to die out or to join the world money economy that generates increasing quantities of consumer products and trash.

It will not be easy to get the people of the United States to reduce their environmentally destructive economic system. Unfortunately, this argument—and indeed, all other moral arguments—have little practical effect on human behavior, at least when compared with causal effects of scarcity and physical necessity. Shortages and high prices are probably the only effective means for downsizing the modern consumerist way of life. The best hope may be that an intractable scarcity of key resources, such as water, petroleum, or sinks for waste and pollution, will occur as soon as possible. The sooner the effects of scarcity can be felt, the sooner people can recognize the need for restraints, and the less severe the consequences will be.

In any case, an exponential growth in the production of material goods and services is impossible in a finite world. At some probably-not-distant time, mankind will have to learn to live on the material resources that the Earth can provide and sustain. It makes no moral sense at all to have children and then bequeath an overcrowded and damaged world for them to live in. The sooner ethical theories are grounded in the environmental principle, the better will be the lot of the future generations of mankind.

5. To Reduce an Excessive Population Is Morally More Difficult than to Reduce Excessive Consumption

An ethics for a finite world must deal with the morally destructive consequences of the increasing world pollution and the collapsing world ecosystem. Indeed, the environmental principle makes it a moral necessity to stop both the expansion of a runaway global economy and the expansion of a runaway world population. Although it is morally obligatory to reduce both, to reduce overpopulation poses a more devastatingly difficult moral problem than to reduce overconsumption.

If ever fuels, food, or pure water should come into short supply, rich nations could cut back on their extravagant use of these resources—overnight, if necessary. This happened in the United State at the start of the Second World War. All of a sudden, people could not buy sugar, oils or fats, gasoline, tires, new cars. Foods were limited. People planted gardens; they put on more clothing and lived in colder houses. They endured hardship. Physical necessity can cause the sudden end of profligate living.

The practical difficulty of reversing the growth caused by a global capitalism dedicated to steady economic expansion will perhaps be more intractable than that of reversing population growth. The beginning stages of scarcity, however, differ in their effects on different nations. Scarcity only causes the citizens of affluent countries to cut back on their extravagant consumption. A similar scarcity in overpopulated and impoverished countries whose citizens are already living at a near-subsistence level causes a cutback in population. In these nations, scarcity causes the heartrending moral problem of deciding who will get a ration of the necessities of life and who will not. It causes people to fight, starve, and die.

In sum, when an impoverished and overpopulated nation confronts scarcity, its population is reduced. A lack of necessities causes people to die. By contrast, when a rich and over-consuming nation confronts scarcity, it has only to reduce its excessive consumption. Thus, scarcity causes a morally devastating crisis for overpopulated nations, but not for overconsuming nations. The moral obligation stands clear: never allow scarcity to arise and to cause moral tragedy.

6. All Citizens Get Coupons for a Year's Ration of Petroleum Fuels

In order to reduce the amount of carbon dioxide pumped into the atmosphere every year, the fossil fuels, especially the gasoline and diesel oil, that each citizen uses must be reduced. Such a reduction might be accomplished by giving to every citizen over sixteen years of age the same ration of fuel coupons. Obviously, many people will not use their full allotment. The proposal is that people be allowed to sell their unused coupons. A market similar to the Wall Street stock market might list the minute-by-minute value of the fuel coupons as supply and demand vary during the day. The wealthy—as well as highly paid professionals, lawyers, and the chief executive officers (CEOs) of major corporations—will, undoubtedly, need to buy extra coupons to get the fuel to run their sport utility vehicles and yachts, and to maintain their affluent lifestyles. The high demand on the part of the affluent might even bid the price of fuel ration coupons up to many times higher than the original cost of fuel. The coupon system would limit the nation's use of fossil fuels to levels that enhance national security and independence. And there might be a significant and beneficial side effect: the high price of coupons may give a large, nongovernmental subsidy to the poor, as well as a financial bonus to all who are frugal in their use of petroleum.

The effectiveness of this proposal must be tested to see if its enforcement costs are minimal and if it reduces the nation's need to import fuels.

7. Taxation Is a Tool
for Attaining Environmental and Societal Goals

As environmentalists have commonly noted, taxation is not just a means for raising governmental funds. It is a two-edged sword. Potentially, its most important function is to attain environmental and population goals. That is, tax what you don't want. Don't tax what you do want.

- In order to encourage employment and to provide a wide diversity of jobs, wages might not be taxed. That is, the income tax might be abolished. In its place, a graduated tax might be placed on total wealth. This change would more accurately reflect the original but now anachronistic justification for the income tax: namely, the ability to pay. Nowadays, ability to pay is not given by earnings but, more importantly, it is given by the total wealth of citizens. To replace the income tax by a wealth tax might have a correlative and beneficial effect: it might reduce the differential between the superrich and the citizens of average or low income. It might limit the amount of money that wealthy individuals spend lobbying congress to support their power and privilege. It might also reduce the quantity of money that is spent for the thirty-second political advertisements that now seem to determine the outcome of elections.

- In order to discourage the use of energy and virgin raw materials, a high extraction tax might be placed on new materials, while there would be no tax on recycled materials. Such taxes may also discourage manufactures from making throw-away products. The lack of a tax on labor would give manufacturers incentives to make durable goods that can be easily repaired because highly taxed virgin raw materials would be relatively expensive, while the untaxed labor to make and repair them would be relatively cheap.

Finally, having no tax on wages may well create new jobs to disassemble worn-out appliances, computers, and machinery. There would be an economic incentive to separate out all the different kinds of plastics and metals contained in discarded products. Recycled materials would then retain a high quality for reuse.

•In order to reduce consumption, especially the consumption of goods and services whose production requires a high input of energy and fuel, the government could use a value-added tax to replace some of the funds lost when the income tax was abandoned. A value-added tax could be selective. It might not be placed on such basic necessities as bulk grains and beans, basic clothing, and simple housing. But it could be retained on ready-to-eat, processed, and packaged foods. Also, it could be graduated to increase in proportion with the greater extravagance and wastefulness of the product or service.

These changes in taxation could reduce environmental stresses. For example, such taxes may well discourage people from buying unnecessary goods and services; they may save fuel and raw materials; they may decrease the amount of trash. They also may discourage profligate spending on luxury accommodations and holiday travel that use vast amounts of natural resources and energy. They may discourage spending on lavish vacation homes, tourist resorts, golf courses, and luxury cars and yachts.

• In order to reduce population, the tax subsidy that supports large families could be eliminated. Bachelors and childless couples would no longer be taxed at the highest rates. In effect, it would change the incentives: it would no longer allow families to reduce their taxes by having more and more children. There would be a financial reward rather than a financial penalty for having no children.

• In order to reduce the amount of carbon dioxide in the atmosphere, a carbon tax (possibly graduated to increase with the quantity and type of fuel) might make it cheaper to develop and to use renewable energy resources from wind and sunlight.

In summary, the expected result of these changes in taxation is to reduce the present environmental stresses. Whatever may be the regressive effects that such taxes incur, they could be offset by a governmental rebate to the poor. Accordingly, both rich and poor would be discouraged from purchasing goods and services that use land, energy, and virgin natural resources. Taxes should be used to create more of what we need—jobs—and less of what we don't need—trash and the waste of energy and virgin natural resources.

8. Government Loans to Students Pay for Public Education; Students Repay Them when They Join the Labor Force

Centuries ago, when America was underpopulated and had vast and unused natural wealth, every extra child and every immigrant were assets to the nation. Under such conditions, the cost of education was correctly borne by the population as a whole. Because the nation as a whole benefited, the nation as a whole paid for the education of all children.

But now America is overpopulated. The evidence that supports this claim is that having used up vast quantities of its own resources, the United States is now importing resources from all over the world in order to maintain its profligate, throwaway, consumer economy. Every person, whether added by birth or by immigration, increases the number of consumers. As a member of the world's most profligate society, every consumer added to the U.S. population buys more consumer goods and services; requires more production at home or increases the imports from abroad; generates more waste and more pollution; adds more carbon dioxide to the atmosphere; and puts a greater burden on the world's already overexploited lands and natural resources. In short, every added person now harms the whole. Under conditions of overpopulation and a shortage of land and resources, education policies need to become context-sensitive, system-dependent. Education policies need to discourage and not subsidize population growth.

The present education system is broken: its increasing administrative bureaucracy is likely to steadily become less effective and more expensive as money is spent for new programs, new buildings, new equipment, new staff, and for higher wages for administrators—while those who have no need and little control over the system pay the increasing costs.

Education may well improve if those who now benefit from free public education—the parents and the children—had to pay the greater share of the costs of education. Perhaps the federal government could underwrite loans to pupils in grade schools, as it now supports loans to students in colleges and universities. The loans would be repaid, perhaps at little or no interest, as students finish school and begin to earn wages. By increasing the cost of raising a family, financial incentives would be placed on parents to reduce the number of their children. Furthermore, when parents and children pay a large share of the costs, they may be encouraged to get their money's worth for their education dollar. They would be far less likely to tolerate the waste, inefficiency, and incompetence that are so characteristic of the present education system. They would be likely to find ways to spend education funds more effectively. Such a system for financing education might well provide incentives for achieving two environmentally necessary ends: reducing population and improving the quality of education.

In addition, parents and children may well find that the present system of compulsory, regimented, centralized mass education thwarts the purpose of education. Pupils may well be able to learn more and to learn more rapidly if all could learn at their own pace, on their own schedules, and according to their interests and the varying stages of their development. They might read books on their own and use computers, taped lectures, and teaching programs. Perhaps they could learn at home, at libraries, or at nearby supervised public computer-learning centers that would not require children to waste many hours a day in school busses that haul them to and from distant public schools. Periodic tests could monitor their progress.

Under this proposal, compulsory, regimented, authoritarian public education might become like compulsory, regimented prison life in that it would be reserved only for those parents and pupils (hopefully, only a few) who cannot live as responsible citizens free of state-imposed coercion. Then, the present school buildings and facilities might be used for counseling, remedial teaching, discussion seminars, lab work, sports, and cultural and social activities. They would become voluntary social and cultural centers, not institutions of confinement enforced by administrators, teachers, police, and truant officers.

Remember that this proposal does not claim to be an a priori certainty or self-evident truth. It cannot be refuted by appeal to valid arguments from universal human rights or to society's need for educated citizens. It cannot be rejected by appeal to traditions that were appropriate only long ago, when the United States was underpopulated and needed immigrants and large families to help develop its resources.

This suggestion may be foolhardy and counterproductive. Limited experiments might be tried out—voluntarily and on a small scale—to see if they produce the intended results. The long-term justification of this change in the financing of education may also be found in its indirect consequences—its tendency to reduce the population and to make education more pleasant and convenient, more varied, more effective, and less expensive.

An additional benefit may be found in removing the property tax from its present role as the primary source of funds for public education. Farmers would no longer be forced to break up their farms and timberlands in order to convert them to the housing developments, manufacturing plants, and shopping centers that pay high taxes. It would also encourage small businesses that would no longer be forced to pay high property taxes to support education. Indeed, tax policies for education must not only be judged by their ability to meet children's educational needs, but also by their ability to support the long-term stability of society and the durability and resilience of the environment. A change in the financing of education may produce a complex of beneficial consequences.

9. Vegetarianism Repairs Environmental Damage and Improves Human Health

As previously noted, E. O. Wilson states that human beings are now using 40 percent of the biomass that the Earth's plants produce by photosynthesis.[7] The human population is predicted to increase to between 9 and 12 billion during the twenty-first century. The near doubling of the human demands on the Earth's plants will leave little photosynthesized energy to support all the other living things on Earth. If the human demand on the Earth's plants increases much more, a severe rationing of all biological resources will be inevitable in order to avoid a worldwide breakdown of the Earth's biological commons.

Between 30 and 90 percent of the food value of grains and beans is lost when these basic foods are fed first to the cows, goats, sheep, pigs, and chickens, and then the animals are eaten as meat.[8] Even now, the world's people are largely vegetarians. Surely, a doubled population can no longer afford to have a meat-based diet.

In the nineteenth century, Americans destroyed one of the world's great ecosystems. It turned the tallgrass prairies of North America into cropland. All the animals of the prairies were killed off, including millions of bison and the carnivores that preyed on them. Aldo Leopold noted that an untold variety of prairie wildflowers and grasses also were lost.[9] Similarly, the decimation of Eastern forests caused the extinction of the millions of passenger pigeons that once darkened the sky for days over the Middle West.

A vegetarian diet would drastically reduce the demand for the grains and beans that are now used to feed our meat animals. By minimizing the need for these basic foods, it would allow the restoration of some prairie lands and some Eastern forests to an original state. Some farmlands—especially land near creeks and rivers—could gradually be returned to an original condition. They could become national parks, available for citizens to find relief from the noise and stress of city life. An additional benefit would be that the lowlands near streams and rivers, which are subject to regular flooding, could become wilderness preserves that would catch the silt that now clogs rivers and estuaries. They also could provide the corridors that would allow the plants and animals to migrate to suitable habitats as the world's climate and rainfall patterns evolve. The result would be to enable American rivers to run clear again.

Over a period of hundreds of years, people could gradually reverse the present pattern of land use. The convention that allows people, governments, and corporations to own all the land of a nation could be changed. Instead of allowing landowners to use and develop all the nation's land (with only small pockets set aside for parks and nature preserves), vast areas would not be owned. The land area that people can own, develop, and live on would become similar to Swiss cheese: the holes would be the land set aside for human ownership and use; the main body of the cheese would be the land returned to a natural state.

Indeed, a vegetarian diet can repair environmental damage and improve human health. It can allow human beings to walk more gently on the Earth.

10. A Significant Causal Link Is Established between Those Who Receive Health Care and Those Who Pay for It

The present system of medical care is broken. It has built-in incentives that keep people from mending their ways. People who abuse their bodies with junk food, alcohol, cigarettes, unprotected sex, and lack of exercise expect others to pay to repair the damage that they have done to themselves. Medical policy cannot ignore the role of causation in human affairs. Ways must be found to assure that people's freedom to abuse their health is causally linked to their responsibility to pay a significant part of the costs of treating the ills they have caused themselves.

For example, tax receipts from liquor, tobacco, and possibly on the junk foods that are full of sugar and fat should not be added to the general governmental funds. Rather, the monies generated by taxes on health-damaging products should be used to pay the added costs of treating the diseases that these products cause. This would reestablish some causal link between those who get health care and those who pay for it.

Surely, medical care must be rationed. Since everyone is going to die of something, those who are near death do not have the same right to expensive medical procedures as those who are young or in the productive years of their lives. There can be no blank check for unconditional health care. No system of health care can survive if health care is the right of all citizens no matter how they abuse their bodies, while the costs of the intensive care they need are borne by people who maintain their health. Medical costs will only rise out of control as long as all citizens have the unconditional right to medical care but no responsibility to pay for it. The right to medical care must be linked to all individuals' obligation to be responsible for their own health.

II. Governmental Offices Sell
Basic Foods at World Wholesale Prices

In order to end the bureaucratic and inefficient system of food stamps and food subsidies, the basic foods—grains, vegetable oils, rice, and beans—might be offered for sale to the public at the low world-export prices of a few cents per pound. No longer could food stamps be used to buy ready-to-eat food loaded with fat and sugar at inflated retail prices. No longer could people privately trade off items purchased with food stamps for liquor, cigarettes, and luxuries.

The basic foods would need to be on sale at public agencies in every town and community. Indeed, there would be costs for distribution and selling involved, but I suspect that the cost would be only a fraction of that of the present food-stamp system.

This proposal would have the advantage of encouraging people to be responsible for preparing and cooking their own food. It would also prevent the poor from wasting their food stamps to buy expensive ready-to-eat foods that often damage their health. It would also give real meaning to philanthropy—if some poor parent asked anyone for ten cents to buy a pound of grain for his or her starving children, few passersby, whether they are idealistic liberals or compassionate conservatives, could refuse the request. The federal government could cut back on an expensive bureaucracy that gives high salaries and job security to those who direct the distribution of food aid to the poor.

A consequent of this proposal would be to get the government out of the business of deciding which citizens to feed and which citizens to allow to go hungry.

12. Advertising Is Curtailed to Reduce Consumption and to Secure a Durable and Resilient Environment

There is much evidence that the present use of land, energy, and biological resources exceeds the amounts that nature can sustain. The health of the environment calls for a drastic reduction in both the throughput of physical and biological resources and the amount of trash that people generate. Hence, the production and sale of material goods and services needs to be greatly curtailed.

Advertising is commonly recognized as inducing people to want and to buy more consumer goods and services. In so far as advertising is a major cause of excessive consumption and waste generation, it is now, or soon will be, as much a threat to the environment as the false cry of "Fire!" in a crowded theater is to the audience. Consequently, experiments are called for to reduce excessive and unnecessary consumption. A reduction in the kind and the amount of advertising may be an effective first step for accomplishing this environmentally necessary task.

Few businesses doubt that advertising promotes the sale of their products, because they spend exorbitant sums of money on it. The money that they spend on advertising supports the claim that advertising makes people want more and buy more. In addition, the very high prices paid for advertising generate the money to pay the exorbitant salaries of sport stars, entertainers, and CEOs of major corporations.

These people then become super consumers who waste land, energy, and material resources in extravagant living. In these ways, advertising now drives the exponential growth of the consumer economy.

In order to reduce the incentives for consumers to want more and to buy more consumer goods and energy-wasting services, the percentage of the advertising costs that are allowed as Internal Revenue Service deductions for business expenses might be decreased year by year, until no such deductions are allowed at all. Then, if advertising still encourages the consumption of goods and services that consume energy and waste natural resources, advertising could be taxed. The effectiveness of these changes will be determined by their ability to reduce the demand for material goods and services and to minimize the trash that people generate.

Admittedly, advertising affects freedom of speech and access to information. But advertising in the modern media contains only a negligible amount of factual data, and much of that is deliberately misleading. Many different experiments could be devised to determine the best way to make necessary information about new products and services available to consumers. Surely, advertising can be curtailed as a means of reducing consumption and of assuring a durable and resilient environment without compromising the public's legitimate right to know.

13. A Nation's Climate and Environment Are Recognized as Affecting Citizens' Behavior

The nations of the world control different amounts of territory and have different soils, climates, and natural resources. Some nations have short days in winter and long days in summer. Others have days of nearly twelve hours all year long. Furthermore, the temperate zones—or at least the zones that have a growing and a dead or fallow season—can generally produce more food and have fewer pests and diseases than the tropics that have year-round growing seasons.

Consider some of the physical differences between the well-to-do, temperate North and the poverty-stricken, tropical South. In temperate climates, winter can be long and severe. Until modern times, people in temperate climates who did not work hard in summer to store food and provide clothing, shelter, and adequate fuel for the winter did not survive. Children did not make it if their parents failed to take care of them through the long, hard winters. Furthermore, few children prospered if their parents did not discipline and train them to meet the challenges and hardships imposed by nature.

Tropical climates present different conditions for life. There are no winters. The discipline that nature demands is more lenient. There is little need for the discipline of storing and preserving food, of constructing elaborate housing, of making clothing, or of collecting and drying firewood. There is little reason to deny instant gratification because food can be grown or gathered year-round, housing can be a simple thatched roof, and children can run outdoors with minimal, if any, clothing or parental guidance. In the tropics, a high birthrate can compensate for a lack of parental care, whereas in temperate zones, high birthrates without necessary parental care are likely only to increase death rates. Indeed, people of the tropics can put off until tomorrow what they could do today.

Unavoidably, tropical environments allow human behavior to differ greatly from the behavior that temperate climates demand. Indeed, there are climatic causes for the lack of discipline, for the high birthrates, and for the poverty and disease found in the tropics. Environmental differences and the behavior that they generate work together to modify the human rights, the moral responsibilities, and the standards of living that are physically possible. Until tropical people learn self-discipline, disease control, and reproductive restraint, nature will continue to limit their rights, freedoms, and opportunities.

Again, it is not the fact that citizens of all nations are human that determines their rights, opportunities, and freedoms. But rather, it is what citizens do, how climates affect their behavior, and what their nation's lands and resources will produce that determines the human rights, freedoms, and opportunities that are possible for them to have.

14. A Low Population Density
Allows a Maximum Quality of Life

People must learn that moral life does not take place in an imaginary world of universal human rights and humanitarian duties. Rather, it takes place in finite and evolving environments whose limited lands and resources determine the narrow window of possible human activity. Furthermore, this window narrows as the increase in population or in economic production steadily degrades the environment. Thus, if ever open land and resources come into short supply, physical scarcity determines the quality of life that citizens may have.

Furthermore, all materially dependent values are conditional and interdependent. The resources that are used to support one cannot support another. To gain one materially dependent value forces the loss of another. The finitude of the renewable resources within every nation's boundaries forces constant trade-offs between the size of the population and the standard of living or the quality of life that citizens can have.

In general, as the population of any nation grows, or as its use of energy and natural resources increases, the harm that people cause each other and the environment increases exponentially. The asymptote toward which life is driven in an increasingly crowded and resource-poor nation is a completely regimented one. It approaches life on a spaceship to Mars, where no significant personal freedoms are allowed and every astronaut's activity is determined by what is physically necessary for the success of the voyage.

Many experiments are possible if nations are allowed to seek their own balance between the size of the population and the quality of life that the renewable resources within the national boundaries can sustain.

At one extreme, some nations or peoples may opt to have a large population and to use the renewable resources within their national boundaries to support a maximal population at a minimal quality of life. They will use almost all the land or resources they have to support their citizens at a bare subsistence level. Little will be leftover to support education, research, medical care, leisure, and the cultural amenities of life.

At the other extreme, some nations may choose to maintain a small population and use most of the renewable resources of the nation to maintain a high quality of life. Citizens can have a varied diet; commute long distances to work; and live in houses with the amenities of running water, refrigerators, central heating and cooling, and indoor bathrooms. Funds will also be available to support education, universities, libraries, research institutions, hospitals and health care facilities, leisure and cultural activities, as well as parks and nature preserves, and the freedom to travel.

As societies become larger and their economic systems more complex and interdependent, the livelihood of citizens depends on the work of others. The ways in which human beings can bother and harm each other increase exponentially. To be specific, as populations become more dense, the noise level of radios and high-fidelity recorders; social gatherings; the city traffic of cars, trucks, busses, and airports; lawn mowers; and even barking dogs and crowing roosters must be controlled. Furthermore, regulations need to be enforced that mandate the construction, wiring, sewage and water systems for private houses; garbage pickup; types of pets that are allowable, and on, and on. Trash burning, parking, and tree removal either require a permit or are prohibited altogether. Furthermore, in order to assure the common welfare, regulations even specify exactly those professionals who are authorized to build or make repairs on private property. By right of eminent domain, governments take private property away from citizens for such public purposes as widening streets or building more schools, libraries, parks, and playgrounds. In short, the greater the size and complexity of any society, the greater the need for governmental control and for ever-higher taxes to cover the costs of the extra services that a growing population requires.[10]

When land and the natural resources of a nation come into short supply, scarcity limits the rights and freedoms its citizens may have. It is physically impossible for the rights and opportunities of the citizens of overpopulated nations to be the same as those of the citizens of nations that maintain a minimal population and limit their use of energy and material resources to quantities that their national boundaries can sustain.

The thesis is simple: trade-offs are inevitable. If citizens want less governmental control, more rights, and greater personal freedom, they must reduce the number of people who can harm and interfere with each other. If they want the comforts of modern living, they must reduce the size of their population and its demands on the nation's lands and natural resources. A low population density maximizes the freedoms and the quality of life that are possible within the finite boundaries of every nation.

15. There Is No Optimal Population and No Correct Way for People to Live in a Finite World

The question "What is the *optimal* human population?" is misconceived. It is similar to asking the question "What is the optimum length of a river?" It is too vague to have an answer.

The belief that there is an optimal population is part of the whole system of mistaken assumptions on which an a priori, egalitarian ethics is founded. As previously noted, the fundamental error of this ethics is to place moral behavior in the abstract domain of thought. There, valid reasoning from a human-centered definition of value and from moral principles that are merely hypotheses is believed to justify moral principles that apply universally and without bias to all mankind. In this domain of thought, the rules of moral life are universal in scope and invariant in their application. They cannot be altered by mere factual contingencies. That is, they cannot change as human moral agents pass from infancy through maturity to old age. They cannot allow the density of a population and the resources of an environment to work together to set the rights, freedoms, and opportunities that are possible for citizens to have. In short, the concept of an optimum population belongs to the imaginary world of thought. It has no relevance to the biological world in which people are born, live, and die; it has no relevance to environments whose support capacities are constantly evolving.

Because cultural evolution is much faster than genetic evolution, modern civilization has developed in a mere moment of geological time. The industrial nations have learned how to exploit all at once the resources that it took the Earth millions of years to create and to sequester. Indeed, the rapid exploitation of natural capital has supported a rapid and unprecedented increase both in the human population and in the production of the material goods and services that sustain the extravagant character of life in the industrial nations. But when the rapid squandering of nature's capital threatens to deplete the world's supply of natural and biological resources, people will have to learn to live within the support capacities of their national boundaries. As noted above in the fourteenth proposal, many compromises are possible between a small population with a maximum of all the amenities of life and a large population living at the minimal level of mere subsistence. In any case, only different experiments will allow the people of different nations to discover how they can have an acceptable quality of life while they preserve the stable and resilient character of the national environment that supports them. By retaining the better and sloughing off the worse, people and nations can gradually find an acceptable compromise between the size of their population and the quality of life that their environment can sustain.

Just as there is no optimal length of a river, there is no optimal population; there is no optimum way of life for all mankind.

16. The Average Workweek Is Reduced

Modern technology constantly invents new, efficient techniques that produce more material goods and services with less human labor. It is high time that the labor-saving benefits of technology should be shared by all. People generally should work less! They should not have to work harder and longer hours in order to buy the ever-greater quantity of consumer goods and services that advertising makes them want and that long hours of work enable them to buy.

In the depression of the 1930s, Bertrand Russell noted the absurdity of having half the citizens work full-time to support the other half—who were either unemployed or worked at wages so low that they needed public assistance. Instead, everyone should have worked fewer hours and shared the employment opportunities.

The beneficial effects of reducing working hours are multiple. One is to help people get their priorities straight. They should buy only what they actually need; they should not buy what advertising and a desperate lack of time makes them buy. Another benefit is that if people work fewer hours, they can become freer by being more self-reliant; they can learn to do the minor household chores and repairs that they have to hire highly paid professionals to do when they work long hours every day; they can also grow and prepare more of their own food. A third benefit is that waste and environmental exploitation can be lessened as workers earn less, need less, and consume less. Fourth, when reduced incomes force people to spend less, the economic system can make a soft landing to steady state; then people no longer will have to work longer and harder to buy more of the unnecessary consumer goods that keep the economy growing.

In addition, to reduce the average workweek furthers

the ideals of democracy. When adequately paid jobs are available to all citizens, none have to work at the low wages that keep them in demeaning poverty. A better distribution of wealth reduces the corporate profits that pay the excessive salaries of corporate officers and that give unearned dividends to stockholders. As citizens learn to satisfy their own basic needs and live more frugally, they can increase their freedom and independence while they further the environmental and human goals of ethics.

17. Unearned Capital Gains Do Not Belong to Individuals; Rightfully, They Belong to Society

When the government has paid the costs of building new infrastructure that new developments require, the capital gains derived from opening up new lands to development belong to society and not to the original landowners, who have made no new investments. Again, when population growth increases the price of suburban property, the capital gains belong to the government that has paid the costs of the new roads, electric plants, sewage systems, schools, parks, and police and fire protection that serve the new residential areas. When such capital gains go to the state, they could be used to reduce other taxes.

Several examples will clarify the proposal:

• When a new access road to the highway system increases the value of nearby land for development manyfold, the capital gains go to the government that has paid the costs of the highway system. They should not go to the original landowner or developer, who has paid little or nothing for the development.

• When the population pressure of citizens who seek new houses in the suburbs raises the price of land from, say, $1000 per acre as farmland to $50,000 or more per acre when it is subdivided into housing lots, the increase in land value goes to defray the costs of the infrastructure needed to serve the new population. Net capital gains should not go to the former owner or to the developer. They belong to the state.

• When a prospector finds a mineral site on federal lands, the sudden multifold increase in value of the site properly goes to the government and not to the prospector or previous owner.

The environmental and moral error of allowing unearned capital gains to go to developers is that it rewards prospectors and entrepreneurs for increasing the exploitation of the world's resources. By contrast, the environmental principle requires a different system of incentives. It does not reward individuals for expanding the exploitation of the Earth's limited resources. It does not allow individuals to increase their personal wealth when they devise new ways to deplete the Earth's finite capital of land, fossil fuels, and natural resources. It does not reward individuals by allowing them to become drones who live in luxurious condominiums, visit lavish resorts, have exotic travel, own yachts, and buy all the adult toys. The environmental principle prohibits all incentives that increase waste and the unnecessary exploitation of land, energy, and resources. It does not allow the wealth from capital to defy the environmental principle by increasing the human exploitation of nature.

18. Invested Money Earns No Interest

According both to medieval European and to present Muslim traditions, interest is immoral. Why?

Material things naturally deteriorate with time. A good apple crop, for example, has less value in the spring than it had in the fall. A ten-year-old roof is less serviceable than a new one. The fall potato crop has little value six months later in the spring. Grain stores deteriorate as insects, mice, and mold take their toll. Maybe the purpose of saving can best be realized when investments merely retain their value?

As David C. Korten states in an article entitled "Economies for Life," the capitalist economy is a suicide economy.[11] It builds on a steady growth in the production of material goods and services. But a finite world cannot supply the energy, the land, and the material resources that capitalism requires to sustain exponential growth. At some time, the capitalist economic system has to become a steady state system, or it will cease to function in this finite world.

It should be the goal of an ethics for a finite world to require an economic system that pays interest only on investments that produce more material goods and services by using fewer raw material and energy resources. The advantage to society of not paying interest on any other types of investment is that almost all citizens will earn exactly what they spend. Those who produce nothing will not be able to live lives of great luxury supported by the work of others. The American dream that everyone can become rich, lazy, and self-indulgent is an illusion. In a steady state economy, wealth and authority can be accorded only to those who make a significant contribution to society; it cannot reward those who merely inherit wealth, or those who find ways to increase their profits or income at the expense of others. Economic systems must curtail and discourage all activities that defy the environmental principle and that diminish the general quality of life. Not to pay interest on invested capital supports the environmental principle and helps realize the goals of moral life.

19. The Environmental Principle
Suggests a Nonegalitarian Conception of Justice

As previously noted, an ethics that builds on the environmental principle recognizes that causation works in human affairs. It acknowledges the need to encourage and reward those who limit their own material needs; who, with their partners or spouses, have only one or two children; who maximize their contribution to society; and who work to preserve the environment. It discourages and even prohibits behavior that subverts the goals of moral life.

An environmental ethics cannot allow an egalitarian definition of justice to assure that all genetically human individuals have the same rights, freedoms, and opportunities and the same access to the necessities of life regardless of what they do. To be specific, ethics cannot reward people for begetting many children whom they cannot support; for their inability to resist the immediate gratification of their desires; for contributing little or nothing to society; or for trashing the environment—while, at the same time, it makes those who act morally take care of all who act immorally. Any ethics that gives a reproductive advantage to those who have defied the environmental and human goals of ethics is a suicide ethics. It cannot long direct the moral behavior of people in a finite world.

Perhaps the conception of justice suggested by Socrates is preferable to one that grants equal freedoms, rights, and opportunities to all. Socrates said that justice means that all people should get what is due them. A modern version of his proposal might be that people's rights, freedoms, and opportunities depend not on their being a member of the human race, but rather on their actions. All should receive greater rewards who work both for their own welfare and for that of society and the environment. All should receive diminished rights, freedoms, and opportunities who do little or nothing for themselves, who harm or burden others, and/or who damage the environment. Ethics cannot make those who act morally support all those who do not. It cannot punish those who advance the goals of ethics while it rewards those who defy them. In short, justice should require that people receive their due. Those who defy the goals of moral life should not have the same rights, freedoms, and opportunities as those who further them.

20. Different Nations and Societies Use Different Methods for Reducing and Controlling Their Populations

The finitude of the Earth limits the human population that the Earth can support. Regardless of the contrary incentives implicit in egalitarian religious and moral beliefs, a finite Earth cannot support an ever-growing human population. Clearly, the human population will someday reach a steady state or it will undergo a population boom and bust.

To those who are not blinded by human arrogance or blinkered by a species narcissism, human beings have become like a plague of locusts. They are consuming every mineral and biological resource that can be put to human use. The nations that have depleted their own resources now rely on global trade and the free-market system to suck in unused resources from all over the world. Market forces and population pressures now fuel a steady economic expansion. They work together to turn more and more of the Earth's resources into consumer goods that end up as pollution and trash.

A major cause of expanding human needs is the constant increase in human numbers. Admittedly, the rate of increase in the human population is decreasing, but because the population base is growing, the total increase remains large: an extra billion people every ten to twelve years, or 200,000 more people every day. The additional people have to live somewhere. Because they are being born, by and large, in impoverished, nonindustrialized countries, they either leave their barren plots of land to go to megacities, or else they emigrate to wealthy industrialized nations. There they simply add to the size of the population that is sucking in fuels, water, and natural resources from all over the world. In effect, the increasing population only furthers the devastation that humankind is working on the world environment.

Again, the discussions of the second, thirteenth, and fourteenth proposals are relevant. Because nations have different cultural, religious, economic, climatic, and moral traditions, they need to be allowed to work out their own solutions for reducing and controlling their population. China, for example, has tried to reduce its population growth by limiting the legal family size. Its government realized that legal sanctions are needed to support reproductive constraint. It tried to prevent unauthorized pregnancies by abortion, if necessary. If a second or third child was born, these children did not have the same rights and the same access to education, health care, and jobs as the first-born or single children. The reason is simple: no government can punish those who obey the law by making them share the limited benefits equally and fairly with those who break the law. Lawbreakers cannot be allowed to keep the gains of their illegal behavior.

Draconian methods of population control may work in China, where citizens have a 4,000-year history of living under authoritarian governments. Obviously, such methods are out of the question for a country such as the United States, which was built on a tradition of individual freedom. In the United States, however, financial incentives and disincentives may prove to be the best means for securing a necessary reduction in population. To start, the tax subsidies for having extra children could be eliminated, and those who have no children could be given tax advantages rather than be required to pay higher taxes. If such changes still are not effective, parents who have three or more children could bear the costs of the health care and education that their extra children require.

To reduce the birthrate in the United States, laws could be written that allow full-time employment for only one parent; the other parent would remain at home to provide care and guidance for their children. Alternatively, both parents could work half-time. This proposal makes parents responsible for the guidance of their children. It contrasts with the present system that allows both parents to work full-time, while it makes the government and public schools provide parental guidance. By default, the present system allows peer pressure at public schools to become the major determinant of children's conduct.

In brief, if parents want to have children, they need to take back from the state the responsibility for developing their own children's values, interests, goals, and norms of conduct.

Inevitably, whether ethics plays an active role in reaching this goal or not, the human population will someday reach a steady state both in its size and the quantity of natural resources that it exploits. However, unless mankind can find a prosperous and humane way down to a sustainable state, nature will impose one. And nature's tactics can be ruthless and brutal. The practical means for discovering a moral steady state system is to follow the suggestion in the second proposal that different nations try out different moral-cultural experiments. Each nation can best discover how to limit and stabilize its own population and devise a steady state system of economic production.

The moral goals, however, remain. The first is to assure that the Earth's system of living things endures and retains its resilience. Then, after nations have learned to live within the physical and biological limits of their national boundaries, the second goal can be implemented: to discover how to make human life in society ever more worth living.

Endnotes

Preface
[1] William B. Dickinson, *The Biocentric Imperative* (Petoskey, Mich.: Social Contract Press, 1999), 133–134.

Acknowledgements
[1] Herschel Elliott and Richard D. Lamm, "A Moral Code for a Finite World," *The Chronicle Review*, 15 November 2002, sec. 2.

Introduction
[1] Garrett Hardin, "The Tragedy of the Commons," *Science* 162 (13 December 1968): 1243–1248.

A Commentary on Important Terms
[1] Charles Ponzi was an impoverished member of the Italian nobility who immigrated to the United States to make his fortune. In 1920, he originated the type of business venture that bears his name. His scheme let him rapidly realize his dream of wealth in the early months of 1920. But his wealth was ephemeral. His scheme appeals to people who want to get rich quickly because it pays a high rate of return. However, it produces nothing. It pays the returns out of the capital that new investors put into the scheme. As long as new money keeps coming in and the business keeps growing, its success is secure. Indeed, it could thrive forever in an infinite world with an infinite number of gullible investors. But it cannot work when the

number of investors is limited. If people stop investing in the venture, it fails. Everyone loses both interest and principal.

Chapter One

[1] Aldo Leopold, *A Sand County Almanac* (New York: Ballantine Books, 1970), 239. The environmental principle has its origin in Leopold's statement "The land ethic simply enlarges the boundaries of the community to include soils, waters, plants, and animals, or collectively: the land."

[2] Jared Diamond, "The Last Americans," *Harpers* 306, no. 1837 (June 2003): 43–51.

[3] Jared Diamond, *Guns, Germs, and Steel* (New York: W. W. Norton & Co., Inc., 1998), 411. Jared Diamond supports the thesis that environmental collapse is the cause of the demise of civilizations. "Thus, Fertile Crescent and eastern Mediterranean societies had the misfortune to arise in an ecologically fragile environment. They committed ecological suicide by destroying their own resource base. Power shifted westward as each Mediterranean society in turn undermined itself, beginning with the oldest societies, those in the east (the Fertile Crescent). Northern and Western Europe have been spared this fate, not because its inhabitants have been wiser but because they have had the good luck to live in a more robust environment with higher rainfall, in which vegetation regrows quickly."

[4] The Editors, "Eating Meat," *WorldWatch* 17, no. 4 (July/August 2004): 12–20.

Chapter Two

[1] John Rawls, *A Theory of Justice* (Cambridge, Mass.: Harvard University Press, 1971), 3.

[2] Ibid., 4.

[3] Peter Singer, *One World* (New Haven, Conn.: Yale University Press, 2002), 185.

⁴ Virginia Abernethy, *Population Politics* (New York: Insight Books, 1993). For a fuller development of this point, see chapter seventeen, "Energy and Carrying Capacity," 249–251.

⁵ Peter Singer, *Writings on an Ethical Life* (New York: HarperCollins Publishing, Inc., 2000), 29–30. In chapter nine, "All Animals are Equal … ," Peter Singer is fully aware of the absurd consequences that result from a literal enforcement of the concept of moral equality. Indeed, it is physically impossible to treat all human individuals identically when the accidental differences between them are factually significant. To replace a literal conception of moral equality, Singer substitutes the equality of consideration.

Singer's substitution, as far as I can see, just pushes their inequality one step farther back. Equal opportunity cannot guarantee equal outcomes. The more able still succeed. The less able lose out. The more able can have satisfying lives. The lives of the less able will be less satisfying.

Many examples can be found that will confirm that equal consideration is irrelevant or baffling and inconclusive. If a boating accident makes it impossible for you to save both your son and your dog, you give your son and your dog equal consideration. You save your son. The fate of the dog is not altered by its having been given equal consideration.

Again, a beggar on the street and the dean are given equal consideration for the presidency of the university. Equal consideration does nothing to change the fact that the nondefining but factual differences between the beggar and the dean determine their fate.

Empirical evidence confirms that the accidental differences between human beings change their prospects for health, longevity, freedom, and personal fulfillment. The best that an equality of consideration can do is to assure that the moral losers do not win and that the morally steadfast do not lose.

⁶ Henri Bergson, *Creative Evolution*, trans. Arthur Mitchell
(London: MacMillan and Co., 1922), 142–174. During
the first part of the twentieth century, Henri Bergson was
a world-famous philosopher. In his book *Creative
Evolution*, he argues that just as Darwinian theory of evolution revolutionizes biology, it revolutionizes philosophy as well. Because everything in nature is evolving,
there is no preordained goal toward which the evolutionary process is directed. Creative novelty, not a timeless
plan, is the essential characteristic of nature.

In chapter two, Bergson explains how evolution
limits the intellect. Concepts and definitions—the basic
tools of reason and the intellect—do not change, whereas
the reality they purport to describe is constantly evolving. There is a mismatch: reason and intellect falsify
nature. For example, the concept of horse changes step
by step from eohippus to modern horse to some future
species. There is nothing permanent in the biological
world for changeless concepts to refer to. The intellect is
merely a tool that Homo sapiens have developed to better
compete in the struggle for survival. It distorts a reality
that constantly evolves toward a state that is being created by the evolutionary process itself.

Bergson's work certainly has to be read critically.
His proposals for understanding reality are nebulous and
untestable. Still, his work has much significance for
ethics because it calls attention to the fact that modern
ethics has not yet come to grips with the Darwinian revolution. Ethics is mired in the pre-Darwinian, Platonic
mindset that assumes that reason and the intellect depict
the timeless structure of the moral world. Accordingly,
this mistaken mindset requires all men and women to be
treated as morally identical because they are all instances
of the same concept. Yet because the concept of human
being is timeless and universal, it cannot give moral significance to the changing yet fundamental differences
that exist between individuals who are genetically

human. However, the fact is that people are not like atoms of hydrogen. One human being cannot be replaced by any other in the application or enforcement of moral laws and principles. Rather, human individuals have different genes, personalities, abilities, ages, and degrees of health, knowledge, and discipline. Although these varying, accidental differences are not essential to the definition of being human, they do cause fundamental differences in what happens to people in the various environments and under the changing circumstances in which they live. To ignore these differences and to draw conclusions about moral behavior that are validly deduced from unconditional moral laws and universal human rights can cause destructive consequences for individuals, for society, and even for the environment.

Just as the geocentric bias of Ptolemaic astronomy caused it to distort the nature of the heavens, so the Platonic bias of Western ethics makes it distort the nature of moral life on Earth. They err because they build on factually false assumptions.

Anyone who can read *Creative Evolution* in the original will be charmed by Bergson's mastery of the French language.

[7] K. S. Shrader-Frechette, "Energy and Ethics," in *Earthbound: New Introductory Essays in Environmental Ethics*, ed. Tom Regan (Philadelphia: Temple University Press, 1984), 126.

[8] Rawls, *A Theory of Justice*, 21.

[9] Richard Hare, *Freedom and Reason* (New York: Oxford University Press, 1963), 1.

[10] Rawls, *A Theory of Justice* 14–15.

Chapter Three

[1] Garrett Hardin, *The Ostrich Factor: Our Population Myopia* (New York: Oxford University Press, 1999), 91.

[2] Ibid., 104.

[3] Garrett Hardin, "Carrying Capacity as an Ethical Concept,"

in *Lifeboat Ethics*, ed. George R. Lucas Jr. and Thomas W. Ogletree (New York: Harper and Row, 1976), 133.

⁴ Elliott and Lamm, "A Moral Code for a Finite World," sec. 2.

⁵ Garrett Hardin, *Stalking the Wild Taboo, Third Edition* (Petosky, Mich.: The Social Contract Press, 1996), 271–274.

⁶ Thomas Hobbes, *The Leviathan*, ed. Richard Tuck (Cambridge, U.K.: Cambridge University Press, 1991). In chapter thirteen of *The Leviathan*, Hobbes wrote that in the state of nature there would be "no arts, no letters, no society, and which is worst of all, continual fear and danger of violent death, and the life of man solitary, poor, nasty, brutish, and short." This is a modification of Thomas Hobbes's famous statement. Obviously, in an impoverished and overpopulated world, life would be crowded, not solitary. Otherwise, it might well be as Hobbes said: poor, nasty, brutish, and short. Inevitably, in a finite world, the quality of human life is a function of the number of people who live in it. When the Earth's biosystem is maintained in an enduring and resilient state, a high quality of life is possible only for a relatively small number of people.

⁷ Aldo Leopold, *A Sand County Almanac*, 117. In the following passage, Leopold suggests that ethics is biocentric: "It is a century now since Darwin gave us the first glimpse of the origin of species. We know now what was unknown to all the preceding caravan of generations: that men are only fellow-voyagers with other creatures in the odyssey of evolution. This new knowledge should have given us, by this time, a sense of kinship with fellow creatures; a wish to live and let live; a sense of wonder over the magnitude and duration of the biotic enterprise."

⁸ E. O. Wilson, *The Future of Life* (New York: Alfred A. Knopf, 2002), 33.

Chapter Four

¹ Abernethy, *Population Politics*, 116.

[2] Herman Daly, "Population, Migration, and Globalization," *WorldWatch* 17, no. 5 (September/October 2004): 41–44.

[3] Diamond, "The Last Americans," 43–51.

[4] Hardin, *Stalking the Wild Taboo,* 271–273.

[5] Ibid., 274. This suggestion, which I am sure most people will find morally abhorrent, follows from Hardin's claim that conscience is self-eliminating. My intent here is only to stress the moral necessity to never allow overpopulation or environmental degradation to entail the moral outrage of altruistic suicide.

[6] Aaron Sachs, "Dying for Oil," *WorldWatch* 9, no. 3 (May/June 1996), 10–12.

[7] Wilson, *The Future of Life,* 33.

[8] For a fuller discussion of the environmental problems caused by meat eating, see the feature article "Eating Meat" by the editors of *WorldWatch* 17, no. 4 (July/August, 2004), 12–20.

[9] Leopold, *A Sand County Almanac,* 48–54.

[10] Abernethy, *Population Politics,* 231. The following passage is apropos: "Taxes (or inflation) have to rise so long as demands for infrastructure multiply, all users contribute to environmental stress, service recipients begin to outnumber taxpayers, and government tries to provide a minimum level of services to everyone. Taxpaying Americans may find that increases in their wages and salaries do not mean much. Real, disposable, personal income, as well as quality of life, are likely to fall because of inflation, rising taxes, and crowding."

[11] Korten, David C., "Economics for Life," *Yes!* 23 (Fall 2002): 13–17.